The One Pot Dinner
Hannah G. Scheel

A NATIONAL GENERAL COMPANY

THE ONE POT DINNER

*A Bantam Book / published by arrangement with
Nash Publishing Corporation*

PRINTING HISTORY

Nash edition published March 1970
2nd printing......September 1970
Bantam edition published July 1971

2nd printing

3rd printing

4th printing

5th printing

6th printing

7th printing

8th printing

CONTENTS

MEATS

BEEF

CHICKEN

VARIETY MEATS

FOREWORD

Back in 1786 Samuel Johnson said: "A man seldom thinks with more earnestness of anything than he does of his dinner."

I wish I had come across that statement sooner than I did, plus many other quotes from the greats of the world, attesting to their interest in food. It would've given a much needed boost to my complexes.

Since my early childhood the family has delighted in recounting two stories referring to my fondness for food. One that after checking into a resort hotel for the summer I had asked in a quavering voice: "But where's the pantry?" The other, that upon seeing some whipped cream left over from dessert, I had nobly offered to finish it off, should nobody else care for it.

With both stories dating back to that nebulous part of a person's childhood made up more of what people tell him than what he can actually remember, I'm really in no state to defend myself or even repudiate these rumors. I can only demur and admit to an early fondness for and interest in food.

Through the years this trait has stayed with me. It survived a traumatic experience in Home Economics when I was almost flunked because I used my hands to shape the hamburger patties. My quoting Shakespeare's line from *Romeo and Juliet* " 'Tis an ill cook that cannot lick his own fingers" was met by the teacher's icy stare. If memory serves me right, it was only because she couldn't face another semester of my experimenting with her recipes that she gave me a passing grade. The art of shaping meat patties with two forks still eludes me, but not my interest in food.

Wholeheartedly agreeing with Samuel Pepys' entry in his 1665 diary: "Strange to see how a good dinner and feasting reconciles everybody," I find that some of my happiest—but also some of my most miserable—moments have been spent cooking for friends. It took an in-depth self-analysis to solve the problem of my sometime misery.

After reading several tomes I came to the conclusion that I was simply not cut out to be an overseer of logistics—the general of an army of pots, all trying to finish cooking at the same time while racing against a meat thermometer in the oven. In spite of carefully worked out timetables, with notes of reminders pinned up all over the house, including such vital items as when to walk the dog, when to shower and when to dress, the many pots would inevitably get the better of me. By the time my guests would be ready to sit down to dinner, I'd be in a panic: nerves frayed, stomach churning and ready to burst into tears.

Once I had hit upon this realization, the solution was easy. Everything into one pot. If I had only one pot to worry about I'd be fine.

With only one pot going I could enjoy my guests. I didn't worry if they showed up late or wanted another drink before dinner. I could cope with a husband who'd walk in quoting Alexander Woollcott: "Let me get out of these wet clothes and into a dry Martini;" and it no longer threw me when guests followed the European custom of bringing flowers for the hostess. The one-pot dinner guaranteed a fairly neat kitchen where I was able to find space for everything before, during and after dinner, including flower arranging.

I suddenly found myself the master of the dinner situation. In today's vernacular, I was able to turn on or off —dinner that is—as it suited *me* . . . not the dinner.

So agreeing implicitly with the philosophy that led Byron to write:

> *That all-softening, overpowering knell*
> *The tocsin of the soul—the dinner bell,*

I started my search for one-pot recipes while serving overseas with the U.S. State Department and continued it after settling down in Hollywood. It has stood me in good stead when serving dinners as well as buffets.

Since in this book I have adhered strictly to recipes that come out of one pot, and in 90% of the cases don't even call for mixing bowls in their preparation, I can only hint at one of my favorite recipes by Alexander Dumas.

In his *Dictionary of Cuisine* he has a recipe for Duck Pâté. After telling you to remove the livers from a dozen ducks, he blithely continues on to instruct you in how to sauté them in a dreamy *beurre* before serving them over eggs to twelve appreciative friends. Not once does he ever refer to the dozen ducks again. Now that's what I call class.

Since desserts aren't my strong point (I prefer cheese and fresh fruit to finish off a meal) you'll have to look elsewhere to satisfy your sweet tooth. But if it's only a tinge of sweet you want after dinner, let me suggest an easy way to accomplish this. Simply add ¼ teaspoonful of cocoa to each cup of after-dinner coffee. It's delicious and enhances the flavor of whatever cognac you might want to sip.

Another quick dessert is made by toasting some shredded coconut in a low, low oven for about five minutes. Sprinkle this over your favorite flavor ice cream—unless it's licorice; pour whatever liqueur you have on hand over it—a coffee- or chocolate-flavored one is best; and, voilà you have a most festive and easy dessert.

As you may have noticed if you've already glanced through the recipes, I use wine a lot; to me it makes that all-important little difference in flavor. And as for accompanying a meal with wine, let me point out to you that the Apostle Paul in his First Epistle to Timothy advised: "Drink no longer water, but use a little wine for thy stomach's sake."

Thomas Moore, the nineteenth-century poet, once said:

> *Though youth gave love and roses,*
> *Age still leaves us friends and wine.*

Even the Greek playwright Aristophanes acknowledged the merits of wine when he exclaimed: "Quickly, bring me a beaker of wine, so that I may wet my mind and say something clever."

Chesterton once described Noah's trials and tribulations during the flood thusly:

> *And Noah he often said to his wife*
> *When he sat down to dine:*
> *"I don't care where the water goes if it*
> *doesn't get into the wine."*

With this point well documented, let's hope I can live up to Cervantes' curt statement: "The proof is in the pudding." On the following pages you'll find some of my favorite culinary experiences, which I'd like to share with you. And do remember the words of George Meredith: "Kissing don't last; cookery do," plus the slight paraphrasing of Byron: "Since Eve served apples, much depends on dinner."

THE ONE POT DINNER

SOUPS

H. L. Mencken was known for going directly to the core of the matter. Who has more honestly described conscience than he when he said: "Conscience is the inner voice that warns us somebody may be looking."

His approach to eating is just as concise and to the point: "To be happy one must be well fed."

Napoleon realized this as well when he said: "An army marches on its stomach."

But in considering the happiness of family and friends, not to mention soldiers, many cooks often neglect one of the most delicious dishes—the homemade soup.

The flavor of that universally popular fish soup, the bouillabaisse, moved Thackeray to write:

> *This Bouillabaisse a noble dish is—*
> *A sort of soup, or broth, or brew.*

What I'm leading up to is simply this: A hearty, home-made soup followed either by a cheese tray or one of your own favorite store-bought desserts is a meal in itself.

Let me show you what I mean.

RICH VEGETABLE BEEF SOUP
(12 Servings)

4	lbs. beef shank with bone
4	qts. water
1	tbs. salt
1	large onion, diced
½	tsp. thyme
½	pkg. *each* frozen green beans, chopped spinach, lima beans, and peas
6	carrots, 1″ pieces
3	cups celery, ½″ pieces
1	green pepper, diced
1	No. 2½ can tomatoes
1	small can whole kernel corn, undrained
2	tbs. parsley flakes
1	pkg. green split pea soup
1	No. 2 can baby onions, drained
¾	cup tomato catsup
1	large potato, cubed

Have the butcher cut the shank in 2″ pieces. Put them into a large kettle, together with the salt, thyme and onion. Add the water, bring to a boil and skim, then let it simmer covered for about 4 hours or until the meat is tender. Remove the meat and bone, cut up meat in bite-size pieces and return to kettle together with all the other ingredients. Simmer for about 30 minutes or until vegetables are done. If you want to, you can make the stock part the evening before or in the morning; bring it to a slow boil about 1 hour before ready to serve, add the vegetables and proceed as above. The soup only improves with reheating.

If I've given you the impression that it's necessary to invite a football team to dinner in order to serve soup, I've led you astray.

A tasty, hearty soup can be fixed in smaller quantities as well, as witnessed by this:

SPANISH VEGETABLE BEEF SOUP
(4 Servings)

1	lb. beef stew meat, cut in 1" pieces
1	veal knuckle
½	lb. chick peas
½	lb. chorizos *or* Italian sausages, sliced
2	qts. water
2-3	beef bouillon cubes
2	cloves garlic, peeled and sliced
½	tsp. crumbled bay leaves
1	tsp. salt *or to taste*
¼	tsp. pepper
2	lbs. potatoes, peeled and quartered
1	lb. fresh spinach

Check the veal knuckle carefully for splinters before putting it into a large pot with all the other ingredients except potatoes and spinach. Bring to a boil, turn down flame and let simmer, covered, for 1 hour and 30 minutes. Add the potatoes and spinach, and simmer for another 30 minutes or until potatoes are done. Remove the veal knuckle and serve soup with crusty sourdough bread.

I once came across an hilarious cookbook entitled *One Arm Cookery*. Its author, Mary Lasswell, had arrived at the title because she believed that the other arm was needed for holding a can of beer. As I recall, though, Miss Lasswell reserved the beer for the cook, never adding it to the food. But with a theory like that, her guests probably had both hands full.

Anyway, a friend of mine goes Miss Lasswell one better. Depending on how thirsty he gets from tasting his soup, he adds a can of beer to his brew just before serving. It does marvelous things for this:

BEERY BORSCHT
(4-6 Servings)

½	lb. beef stew meat
½	lb. lamb stew meat
7	cups cold water
2	med. beets, peeled and diced
1	carrot, ½″ pieces
1	cup celery, diced
1	cup canned tomatoes
½	tsp. ground nutmeg
3	beef bouillon cubes
1	tsp. salt
1	med. onion, diced
2	slices cooked bacon, minced
½	tbs. flour
1	tbs. parsley flakes
1	cup shredded white cabbage
2	large potatoes, peeled and cubed
3-4	slices rye bread, crumbled
1	egg yolk
1	can of light beer
	Sour cream

Cut the pieces of stew meat into halves and put them into a large pot with the water, diced beets, carrots, onion, celery and canned tomatoes. Add the bouillon cubes, nutmeg and salt. Mix the minced bacon with flour and parsley and add to the pot. Stir well, cover and bring to a boil. Lower the flame and simmer for 2 hours. Add the potatoes and cabbage and continue simmering for another 30 minutes.

Just before you're ready to serve, pour a little of the soup into the slightly beaten egg yolk before you add the beer to this mixture. Add the crumbled rye bread to the soup together with the beer mixture. Stir and cook for another 3 minutes, making sure the egg doesn't curdle. Serve with dollops of sour cream on top and make sure you have additional frothy, chilled beer on hand, as well as slices of rye bread and sweet butter.

Culinarily speaking, the Danes are mostly known for their open-faced sandwiches and pastries—which in Denmark, incidentally, are called Viennese pastries—but they don't limit themselves to these items.

Forced by a climate that for at least eight months out of the year is downright chilly, they've found that soup is an excellent way to restore normal temperature to the human body. They further this process by serving the national liquids—beer and aquavit—as accompaniments.

DANISH CABBAGE SOUP
(6 Servings)

2½	lbs. brisket
1	lb. oxtails
10	cups cold water
1	tsp. sweet basil
1	tsp. caraway seed
½	tsp. dill seed
10	whole peppercorns
1	tsp. salt
6	carrots, 1″ pieces
4	potatoes, peeled and quartered
2	leeks, 1″ pieces
6	small white onions, peeled
1	tbs. parsley flakes
2	med. heads white cabbage, in wedges

Put into a large pot the brisket and oxtails, add herbs and spices, cover with water, bring to a boil and then simmer for 2 hours, covered, over low flame. Fish out the pieces of oxtail, add all the vegetables and continue simmering for another 45 minutes. When ready to serve, place the sliced brisket on a separate platter so your guests can make their own open-faced sandwiches with Danish pumpernickel, butter and mustard. The most legitimate kind of Danish pumpernickel is the one sold in your grocer's delicatessen under the name of "Rugbord."

Since the oxtails lend their own saltiness to the soup, don't add more than 1 tsp. salt at the beginning. You can always correct the soup to your personal saltiness just before serving.

If an unfortunate but not too uncommon dislike for cabbage kept you from trying the above Danish way with a soup, do take advantage of their hearty approach to the generally popular barnyard fowl, the chicken.

DANISH CHICKEN SOUP
(4-6 Servings)

4	lbs. stewing chicken, disjointed
2	tsp. salt
½	tsp. pepper
½	tsp. sweet basil
½	tsp. thyme
2-3	chicken bouillon cubes
8	cups cold water
4-6	med. carrots, 1″ pieces
4	leeks, 1″ pieces

Place the chicken pieces in a large kettle, sprinkle with the salt, pepper and herbs, add the bouillon cubes and water and bring to a boil; turn down flame and simmer for 1 hour and 30 minutes.

While the chicken is simmering, clean and cut the vegetables and fix:

MEATBALLS

1	lb. ground beef
¾-1	cup milk
1	med. onion, grated
¼	tsp. pepper
1	tsp. salt
⅓	cup flour
1	egg

Have the butcher run the ground meat through the meat grinder an extra time. Put the meat in a medium-size mixing bowl and add all other ingredients, going easy on the milk, so that the meat mixture doesn't get too soupy.

When the chicken is done, remove it from the soup, skim off any excess fat and add the prepared vegetables. When the soup has reached a fast simmer, drop small balls of the meat mixture from a teaspoon into the soup, letting them simmer for 45 minutes.

About 30 minutes before you're ready to serve the soup make:

DUMPLINGS

1½	cups sifted all-purpose flour
2	tsp. baking powder
¾	tsp. salt
1	tbs. sugar
¼	tsp. ground cardamon
1	egg, well beaten
2	tbs. melted butter
1	cup milk

Sift the flour, baking powder, salt, sugar and ground cardamon into a medium-size bowl. In the measuring cup you use to melt the butter in, mix the well-beaten egg with the milk and pour it into the dry ingredients, stirring lightly until batter is no longer lumpy.

Drop the batter by rounded tablespoonfuls into the simmering soup and cook, uncovered, over low heat for 10 minutes. If you like a real thick soup you can add the boned, cooked chicken; otherwise save it for chicken salad the next day.

If you feel guilty about asking for seconds or thirds of this dish, just remember Ambrose Bierce's consoling words: "Self-denial is indulgence of a propensity to forego."

Let's face it. Scotland is primarily known for its Scotch, its kilts, its bagpipes and its *haggis*—the latter a dish I once thought was made out of the bagpipes and never have been able to develop a taste for. However, the Scots do something to a chicken that deserves more than just a nodding acquaintance.

COCK-A-LEEKIE
(4 Servings)

6	leeks, 1″ pieces
3-4	chicken breasts
3-4	chicken thighs
5	cups water
2	cans chicken broth
1	tsp. salt
¼	tsp. ground nutmeg
12	pitted prunes

Wash the leeks carefully and cut them into 1″ pieces discarding the tough green tops. Place half the leeks in bottom of pot, arrange the chicken pieces on top and cover with the remaining leeks. Sprinkle with salt, nutmeg, pour water and chicken broth over and bring to a boil. Turn flame down and simmer until chicken is tender, for about 45 minutes. Remove the pieces of chicken, add the prunes to the soup and as soon as the chicken is cool enough to handle, pull the meat off the bones and return to soup. Serve as soon as everything is heated through.

Warm hard-crust dinner rolls go well with this, especially if you recall A.A. Milne's plea:

> *Nobody, my darling*
> *Could call me*
> *A fussy man—*
> *BUT*
> *I do like a little bit of butter*
> *To my bread.*

It wasn't until I'd been introduced to the foods of the Near East that I realized lamb could be served in more ways than just as chops, roasts and a leftover sandwich. Once you become aware of this, it's amazing the number of dishes you find enhanced by its flavor. Try this:

MIDDLE EASTERN LAMB SOUP
(4 to 6 Servings)

1	large onion, chopped
2	tbs. olive oil
2	tbs. butter *or* margarine
1½	lbs. lamb stew in 1″ pieces
1	6 oz. can tomato paste
½	cup dry white wine
1	15 oz. can tomato sauce
1	tsp. salt
¼	tsp. white pepper
2	10 oz. pkgs. frozen green beans
3½	cups water
2	beef bouillon cubes
⅛	tsp. ground cumin *or* to taste

While you're sautéing the onion in the olive oil and melted butter, cut the stew meat in 1″ pieces. When the onion is slightly brown, rather than just translucent, add the meat and brown it well on all sides. Now add the tomato paste, wine, tomato sauce, salt and pepper, and simmer for about 45 minutes or until meat is fork tender. Add the beans, water, bouillon cubes and cumin, and simmer for an additional 30 minutes, before you serve. If there's a grocery store specializing in foreign imports in your neighborhood, melba toast with thin slices of feta cheese—the Greek goat's milk cheese—go very well with this soup.

There was a time when no self-respecting Swedish housewife would dream of not serving her family home-made pea soup at least once a week. Although she now may avail herself of either frozen or canned versions, as may you, I do suggest you follow her traditional recipe at least once or twice during the cold season. It's the kind of dish that could have moved Edmund Bentley to write:

> *Sir Christopher Wren*
> *Said "I'm going to dine with some men.*
> *If any body calls*
> *Say I'm designing St. Paul's."*

NOTES

SWEDISH YELLOW PEA SOUP
(4-6 Servings)

1	lb. quick-cooking, dried yellow split peas, washed
3	qts. boiling water
½	tsp. crumbled bay leaves
2	lbs. pork shoulder
1	large onion, chopped
2	tsp. salt
½	tsp. pepper
½	tsp. dill weed
2	leeks, 1″ pieces
1	celeriac, peeled and cubed
1-2	potatoes, peeled and quartered

Combine the washed peas, boiling water and crumbled bay leaves in a large kettle. Bring the mixture to a boil, then reduce the heat and let it simmer for 1 hour, stirring occasionally.

Then add the pork, together with the chopped onion, the salt, pepper and dill, and continue simmering under cover for another hour, before you add the leeks, celeriac and potatoes. In about 45 minutes the vegetables should be done along with the meat and peas.

Remove the meat from the soup, slice on separate platter, and serve with rye bread and butter.

If you want to be a little more fancy, you might want try this variation—both, however, should be served with chilled beer and aquavit if you want to stay in the Scandinavian tradition.

HEARTY GREEN PEA SOUP
(6-8 Servings)

1	lb. quick-cooking green split peas
3	qts. water
1½	tbs. salt
½	tsp. pepper
¼	tsp. allspice
¼	tsp. marjoram
2	beef bouillon cubes
2	lbs. spareribs, in sections of two
2-3	thick leeks, 1″ pieces
1	large onion, sliced
1	cup celery, ½″ pieces
1	lb. smoked sausage
3-4	carrots, ½″ pieces

About 3 hours before you plan to serve dinner, place the peas and water in a large kettle, bring to a boil, and let simmer, covered, for 1 hour and 15 minutes.

Add the salt, pepper, allspice, marjoram, bouillon cubes and trimmed spareribs and stir well. Bring back to boiling before reducing heat to let the soup simmer for an additional 45 minutes, during which time you can wash and cut the leeks into 1″ pieces, cut the onion into thin slices and wash and slice the celery. Add the vegetables and smoked sausage to the soup, allowing it to simmer for another 30 minutes after it has come back to a boil. During the last 15 minutes of cooking add the carrots. Just before serving, ladle out the spareribs and sausage. Pull the meat off the ribs and return to soup together with the thinly sliced sausage.

Serve in deep soup bowls with croutons on hand for those who like to sprinkle them on top.

Before I go into pure vegetable soups, let me give you another recipe from the Near East. Although it calls for some spices you might not have on hand, it would be good to get them—not only for this soup, but for a lot of other dishes. What Logan Pearsall Smith said about writing, "What I like in a good author is not what he says, but what he whispers," applies equally well to these spices.

NOTES

YEMENITE SOUP
(6-8 Servings)

2-3	lbs. boneless veal, cubed
8	cups water
1	clove garlic, minced
1	med. onion, quartered
1	green onion
2	tomatoes, halved
1-2	tsp. salt
½	tsp. pepper
2	tsp. *each* ground coriander, tumeric, cumin and fenugreek
1	Italian parsley root, scraped
1	tbs. parsley flakes
2	zucchini, halved crosswise
2	large carrots, in chunks
½	cup raw rice
3-4	potatoes, peeled and cubed

In a large kettle bring the water to a boil, add the veal and let it simmer, covered, for 30 minutes, skimming it two or three times. Now add the garlic, the quartered onion, whole green onion, tomato halves, salt and pepper along with all the other spices, parsley root and parsley flakes. Bring again to a boil and let simmer for 20 minutes before you add the zucchini, the carrots, rice and potatoes. In another 30 minutes after the soup is back to simmering, it should be ready to serve.

If you want to, you can make this in two steps, starting it the evening before. The best breaking point is before you add the zucchini and what goes with it.

The next two recipes call for no meat. The first one hails from Provence—to many the center of good cooking. If fresh vegetables are available, do use them all along down the line; if not, use a package each of frozen green beans and peas.

With the Provençal soup I must honestly suggest that you follow it with a hearty dessert or you might find yourself reciting Christopher Morley's nursery rhyme:

> *Timid roach, why be so shy?*
> *We are brothers, thou and I.*
> *In the midnight, like thyself,*
> *I explore the pantry shelf.*

VEGETABLE SOUP PROVENCAL
(3-4 Servings)

1	cup fresh string beans *or* 1 10 oz. pkg. frozen
1	cup shelled fresh peas *or* 1 10 oz. pkg. frozen
1	leek, thickly sliced
1	carrot, thickly sliced
½	med. head white cabbage, sliced or shredded
2	potatoes, sliced
1	large tomato quartered
2	qts. water
2-3	beef bouillon cubes
2	tsp. salt
1	pinch cayenne
1	tsp. sweet basil
¾	cup elbow macaroni
	Parmesan cheese

Put everything but the elbow macaroni and Parmesan cheese into a pot. Bring to a boil, reduce heat and let simmer, under cover, for 20 minutes. Add the macaroni, lower the heat and simmer for another 12 minutes, making sure the macaroni doesn't stick to the bottom.

Just before serving sprinkle with Parmesan cheese and have some more ready for those who want a heavier touch of it. Buttered sourdough bread is good with this.

Even if you already have a favorite and trusted recipe for minestrone, try this one. It's just a little bit different from the more popular version and deserves investigation.

MINESTRONE A LA LLUBA
(6 Servings)

⅓	cup olive oil
3	med. onions, chopped
1	celery heart, outer leaves removed, chopped
4	tbs. parsley flakes
1	6 oz. can tomato paste
2	cans beef broth
8	cups water
2-3	beef bouillon cubes
2	carrots, sliced
2	tsp. salt
½	tsp. pepper
⅛	tsp. sage
½	tsp. rosemary
1	small head cabbage, shredded
1	1 lb. can kidney beans, drained
1	med. zucchini, sliced
1	10 oz. pkg. frozen green beans
1	cup elbow macaroni
	Parmesan cheese

Heat the oil in your Dutch oven. Add the onion, celery and parsley and sauté until tender and onion is translucent. Stir in tomato paste, beef broth, water, bouillon cubes, carrots, salt, pepper, sage and rosemary. Bring to a boil, reduce heat and simmer, covered, for 45 minutes before you stir in the drained kidney beans, the sliced zucchini, beans and macaroni. Continue cooking, over low flame so the macaroni doesn't stick, until all is heated through —a good 20 minutes. Serve with Parmesan cheese on the side and thick slices of garlic bread you've prepared during the last 15 minutes of cooking.

Izaak Walton, the father of *The Compleat Angler,* wrote about his favorite pastime: "All that are lovers of virtue, and dare trust in His providence, and can be quiet, go a-angling."

Benjamin Franklin had a rather different view when he dryly commented: "A fishing rod is a stick with a hook at one end and a fool at the other."

Whatever your personal reaction to fishing may be, there's no doubt that the end result has brought many delicacies to the table. In the soup department, the bouillabaisse is probably the best known. The following recipe seems to have taken its inspiration from Thackeray's poem:

> *This Bouillabaisse a noble dish is—*
> *A sort of soup, or broth, or brew,*
> *Or hotchpotch of all sorts of fishes,*
> *That Greenwich never could outdo;*
> *Green herbs, red peppers, mussels, saffron,*
> *Soles, onions, garlic, roach, and dace;*
> *All these you eat at Terre's tavern*
> *In that one dish of Bouillabaisse.*

BOUILLABAISSE
(6 Servings)

¼	cup olive oil
1	clove garlic, minced
1	onion, sliced
1	carrot, sliced
1	tbs. parsley flakes
¼	tsp. fennel seeds, crushed
1	tsp. saffron
2	tsp. salt
¼	tsp. rosemary
1	lb. halibut steak, diced
1	lb. swordfish, boned and diced
2	cups bottled clam juice
2	cups water
¼	cup tomato paste
1	can whole clams (12)
½	lb. lobster meat
½	lb. jumbo shrimp, shelled
1	10 oz. can mussels
¼	cup dry white wine

In a large kettle heat the oil. When it's hot, add the garlic, onion, carrot, parsley and fennel. Sauté until golden, then add the saffron, salt and rosemary. Stir slightly and place a layer of diced halibut on top, followed by a layer of swordfish. Mix the tomato paste with the clam juice and water and pour all over. Cover and simmer for 15 minutes. Add the clams, with liquid, and simmer for an additional 10 minutes. During the last 5 minutes add the lobster meat, the raw shrimp and the canned mussels with their liquid. Just before you're ready to serve, stir in the white wine and carry proudly to the table which is set with deep soup bowls and pretty wine glasses for the chilled white wine you serve with it.

You can do all the cleaning and dicing in advance and keep the ingredients in the refrigerator, but I wouldn't recommend starting to cook the Bouillabaisse until an hour before you plan to serve it.

The long, thin French breads known as "flutes" are ideal with this; otherwise, hard-crust dinner rolls will be fine.

What does the Caribbean conjure up in your mind? Exotic rum drinks, moonlit nights, sensual music and happy flirtations? That's certainly what the ads stress, and let's hope it's true for all those heading that way; but the Caribbean also offers exciting ingredients and tasty recipes.

CARIBBEAN FISH SOUP
(6 Servings)

½	cup olive oil
2	med. onions, chopped
2	lbs. haddock, cubed
1	lobster, shelled and cut in pieces
1	cup raw rice
4	med. potatoes, peeled and cubed
2	large tomatoes, in wedges
2	cups shredded cabbage
2	tbs. tomato paste
7	cups boiling water
3	cups dry white wine
3	pimentos, thinly sliced
2	tsp. salt
½	tsp. pepper
½	tsp. oregano

Heat the oil in a large kettle and add the onions; sauté them for 5 minutes or until translucent. Add the boned, cubed haddock, together with the lobster pieces and rice, and cook over high heat for 5 minutes, stirring constantly. Now add the potatoes, tomatoes, cabbage, tomato paste, boiling water, wine, pimentos, salt, pepper and oregano; stir well, turn down heat when it boils and let simmer for 30 minutes.

Serve in deep soup bowls, accompanied by chilled wine and hard-crust rolls, to guests who might have whetted their appetites on a nice, dry daiquiri.

The remaining soup recipes all use as a major ingredient milk, the juice that according to E. M. Root comes from: "God's jolly cafeteria, designed with four legs and a tail."

The soups may all be started in advance, but to be on the safe side you should always stop your precooking before adding the milk. The first recipe may not look like much, but let me assure you it's been my most trusty stand-by for years.

Sam Goldwyn is reported to once have said: "If you can't give me your word of honor, will you give me your promise?"

I'll back up the Potage with both.

NOTES

POTAGE
(4 Servings)

3-4	large potatoes, peeled and sliced
3-4	large leeks, washed and sliced
¼	cup butter or margarine
3-4	cups water
3	beef bouillon cubes
1	tsp. thyme
1	tsp. salt
¼	tsp. pepper
1	qt. milk, whole

In a pot, sauté the cleaned and sliced leeks in the melted butter until golden, translucent and limp, but not brown. Add the potatoes, bouillon cubes, thyme, salt and pepper, and pour the water over, just enough to cover. Bring to a boil, then reduce heat and simmer for about 35 minutes or until potatoes are beginning to break. Add the milk and bring the soup just to boiling. This takes about 10-15 minutes.

Serve with slices of cheese bread you've heated in a slow oven, followed by fresh fruit, and I think you will agree with Fielding when he said:

> *A little dish oft furnishes enough*
> *And sure enough is equal to a feast.*

The following recipes are basically variations on a theme, although different enough to stand on their own.

PENNY PINCHING CHOWDER
(4-6 Servings)

4	slices bacon
6	frankfurters, sliced
2	med. onions, sliced
4	med. potatoes, peeled and sliced
1	1 lb. can whole kernel corn, undrained
2	tsp. salt
1	tsp. thyme
1	can beef broth
½	tsp. pepper
½	tsp. caraway seed
1	beef bouillon cube
½	cup dry white wine
1	cup water
2	cups milk

In the bottom of a heavy pot, brown the bacon; when done, remove and drain on paper towel. Add to the bacon drippings the sliced onion and frankfurters and brown slightly. Stir in the sliced potatoes, the undrained corn, salt, pepper, thyme, caraway seed, bouillon cube, beef broth and water. Simmer covered, for 30 minutes after it's been brought to a boil. When the potatoes start to break, add the wine and milk and heat *just to boiling;* serve with the bacon sprinkled on top.

I've served this with great success to teen-agers, who gobbled it up along with buttered sourdough bread.

BACON AND CHEESE CHOWDER
(4-6 Servings)

½	lb. bacon, sliced
1	med. onion, chopped
¾	cup celery
3	potatoes, peeled and sliced
2	carrots, sliced
1	lb. chopped broccoli
1	cup water
1	tsp. dill weed
1	tsp. salt
½	tsp. pepper
1	qt. milk
1	cup shredded Cheddar cheese

Brown the bacon in the bottom of a pot; when done remove and drain on paper towel; add the chopped onion to the drippings, letting them brown slightly. Add the celery, potatoes, carrots and broccoli; sprinkle with dill, salt and pepper and pour the water over to cover the mixture. Bring to a boil, reduce heat and let simmer for 30 minutes. Stir in the milk and just before the soup reaches the boiling point, stir in the cheese; continue simmering until it's melted. Serve with crumbled bacon on top accompanied by rye bread and butter. Beer goes very well with this.

MARTHA JANE'S SEAFOOD CHOWDER
(4-6 Servings)

2	leeks, washed and sliced
2	med. potatoes, pared and sliced
1	large green pepper, cut into strips
2-3	tbs. butter or margarine
1	cup bottled clam juice
1½	cups water
1	tsp. dill weed
½	tsp. thyme
½	tsp. salt
½	tsp. pepper
1	12 oz. pkg. frozen scallops
10	jumbo shrimps, shelled
1	7½ oz. can chopped clams
1	qt. milk
2	med. tomatoes, in wedges
½	cup sherry

Sauté the leeks and green pepper in melted butter until leeks are translucent, about 5 minutes. Add the sliced potatoes, dill, thyme, salt and pepper, and pour the clam juice and water over it. Bring to a boil, reduce heat, and simmer, covered, for about 45 minutes. Add the milk, and about 5 minutes later, the defrosted scallops, the raw shrimp, the chopped clams and the tomato wedges. Just before the chowder reaches boiling, stir in the sherry and serve, accompanied by hard-crust rolls and a chilled white wine.

SEAFOOD CHOWDER
(8 Servings)

¼	cup butter or margarine
¼	cup minced onion
2	leeks, thinly sliced
2	cups chicken broth
1	heart of celery, diced
3	carrots, sliced
1	tsp. salt
¼	tsp. pepper
½	tsp. crumbled bay leaves
½	tsp. thyme
½	lb. haddock, cubed
3	cups milk
1	cup light cream
1	cup flaked crabmeat
1	7½ oz. can clams

In a large pot melt the butter or margarine, add minced onion and sliced leek, and sauté until limp and translucent. Pour chicken stock over and add celery, carrots and haddock together with seasonings. Cover and simmer for about 30 minutes before adding the cleaned crabmeat, the can of clams *with liquid,* milk and light cream. Heat just to boiling and serve with crusty rolls.

I once lived in an apartment building owned by a Russian lady. Due to the transient status of many Hollywood tenants, she'd show up on the hour the rent was due, but she was there just as quickly when you were ill.

She knew only two remedies: chicken soup when you were critically ill, and this chowder when the fever had subsided.

I hate to tell you how many times I thought of reverting to the thermometer-in-the-tea trick to rate her services. There was nothing better than lying in bed and being served a steaming bowl of her chowder.

NOTES

RUSSIAN FISH CHOWDER
(4 Servings)

¾	lb. cod, haddock or other firm white fish fillets
1	cup water
4	thin slices smoked salmon
1	tbs. tomato puree
2	tbs. butter
6	cups bottled clam juice
2	tbs. sour gherkins, minced
1	tbs. capers
½	cup cooked shrimp, diced
1	tbs. parsley flakes
1	cup heavy cream
2	tbs. flour *optional*
	Salt and pepper *to taste*

Poach white fish in water for 5 minutes; scoop out and reserve, cutting into bite-size pieces when cool enough to handle. In the same water, cook the salmon for 1 minute before cutting into 1″ squares. Dilute the tomato puree in the fish stock, stir in butter and slowly bring to a boil. Add your precooked fish and salmon together with the clam juice, sour gherkins and capers. Heat it all through before adding the shrimp and heavy cream. If you prefer a thicker chowder, add 1-2 tbs. of flour at the time you stir in butter, stirring well until it thickens.

The next two recipes are for the think-ahead cooks who keep a certain number of staples on hand, making it possible to cope with unexpected guests or to stay snug inside on rainy days instead of having to go and forage for the family. They both use that ever-popular tuna as a main ingredient but give it more personality than usual.

CURRIED TUNA CHOWDER
(4 Servings)

3-4	large potatoes, peeled and cubed
2	10 oz. cans cream of celery soup
1	12 oz. can whole kernel corn
1	small can green peas
¼	cup evaporated milk
1	tbs. instant onion
¼	tsp. white pepper
1	7 oz. can chunk tuna, drained
1-2	tsp. curry
1	tsp. salt

Cook the potatoes until tender in just enough water to cover. Drain off liquid into measuring cup, adding enough water to make 1 cup. Return liquid to pot together with the two cans of soup, the can of peas *with liquid,* the whole corn *with liquid,* the evaporated milk, the instant onion and salt and pepper. Bring to a boil, reduce heat and simmer for about 5 minutes. In a cup blend a little of the soup with the curry and return paste to soup together with the tuna, *drained,* breaking it into small pieces with a fork. Heat through and serve with rolls.

TUNA CHOWDER
(4 Servings)

2	7 oz. cans chunk tuna
1	large onion, sliced
1	12 oz. can whole kernel corn
1	1 lb. 13 oz. can tomatoes
¼	tsp. fennel seed
1	tsp. mustard
¼	tsp. dried basil
½	tsp. dill weed
1	qt. milk
	Salt and pepper *to taste*

Drain the tuna and reserve ¼ cup of oil. Break tuna into pieces. In a pot heat the oil, add the onion, and sauté until tender and translucent. Add the broken-up tuna, the corn *with liquid,* the tomatoes *with liquid,* the spices and herbs. Bring to a boil, reduce heat and simmer, under cover, for about 30 minutes, giving it an occasional stir. Add the milk slowly and heat to just before boiling. Serve with rolls in deep bowls that'll set off the pretty pinkish color of this soup.

This next recipe is delicate in flavor and coloring and just great to serve after you've returned from an early movie. It should be accompanied by a light, chilled white wine and thin bread sticks.

VEGETABLE CLAM CHOWDER
(4 Servings)

2	tbs. butter or margarine
6	scallions, sliced
3	med. potatoes, thinly sliced
¾	cup dry white wine
1	7 oz. can minced clams
1	7 oz. can green peas
2	med. carrots, diced
1½	cup light cream or milk
½	tsp. dill weed

Sauté the sliced scallions in butter for about 5 minutes. Add the thinly sliced potatoes, wine, the liquid from the clams and peas, dill weed and salt *to taste*. If the liquid doesn't cover the potatoes, add just enough water to make sure it does. Cover and simmer for about 25 minutes. Now add the peas and clams together with the milk or cream. Heat to just before boiling, stirring in the clams during the last couple of minutes.

Lord Byron took a very dim view of the fisherman and his activities as attested to by the following poem, lashing out at the father of *The Compleat Angler:*

> *And angling too, that solitary vice,*
> *Whatever Izaak Walton sings or says:*
> *That quaint, old, cruel coxcomb in his gullet*
> *Should have a hook,*
> *And a small trout should pull it.*

However, Walton's fondness for fishing was supported
by Thomas d'Urfrey who wrote:

> *Of all the world's enjoyments*
> *That ever valued were,*
> *There's none of our employments*
> *With fishing can compare.*

Since I have never even considered going fishing, I
shall not take sides in this poetic battle, but only mention that a lot of savory dishes depend on the sea and
the fisherman for their mainstay, such as the following
four recipes.

Being somewhat thicker than the regular soup or
chowder, they are categorized as stews. However, I do
suggest you serve them in soup bowls. The Cioppino is
the Italian cousin of the Bouillabaisse and the others, dis-
tant relatives.

CIOPPINO
(6 Servings)

1½	lbs. halibut steak
1½	lbs. salmon steak
1½	lbs. swordfish steak
3	slices bacon, finely diced
1	med. onion, diced
1	clove garlic, minced
½	tsp. sweet basil
3	tbs. olive oil
¾	cup dry red wine
2	17 oz. cans Italian tomatoes
⅓	cup red wine vinegar
3	tbs. fresh parsley
1-2	tsp. salt
½	tsp. pepper

Carefully cut away all skin from fish steaks and re-move flesh from bones. Cut flesh into 1″ squares and sprin-kle generously with salt.

Sauté the bacon, onion, garlic and basil in heated oil until onion turns yellow. Add the wine, tomatoes, vinegar and parsley; bring to a boil, reduce heat and simmer for 5 minutes. Season to taste with salt and pepper. Add the prepared fish, stirring it once or twice to make sure it's all covered with the sauce before you cover the pot and let the mixture simmer for another 10 minutes. Serve with rolls and accompanied by a dry, chilled vin rosé.

One more thing. If you're figuring on an angling hus-band to bring home the main ingredients for this dish, remember it's a smart cook who keeps some steaks in re-serve for such occasions.

The following recipe combines characteristics of the cooking from most of the countries surrounding the Med-iterranean; thus its general name.

MEDITERRANEAN FISH STEW
(6-8 Servings)

3	large onions, sliced
1	large green pepper, cut in strips
1	1 lb. can tomatoes
1	large leek, diced
2	carrots, sliced
2	tbs. salt
1	tsp. thyme
½	tsp. fennel seed
¼	tsp. black pepper
1	6 oz. can tomato paste
¼	cup olive oil
2	tbs. chili sauce
2	tbs. anchovy paste
1	tbs. lemon juice
2	lbs. scallops, without shells
2	lbs. halibut, boned and skinned

In a large pot combine the sliced onion, pepper strips, undrained tomatoes and diced leek and carrots with the salt, thyme, fennel and pepper.

In a small bowl combine the tomato paste, olive oil, chili sauce, anchovy paste and lemon juice, stirring it well before pouring it over the vegetables. Stir everything well before bringing the mixture to a boil; reduce heat and simmer, covered, for about 15 minutes.

Cut the boned and skinned halibut into bite-size pieces, cut the scallops in halves if very large. Add the fish to to the vegetable mixture and continue simmering, under cover, for another 15 minutes.

Serve with hot, buttered French bread and a good, chilled white wine.

This next Spanish version of the fish stew is a little more elegant and fanciful—calling for wine as well as brandy. But as Grace Lawson said about her recipe for champagne-filled watermelon, domestic brands may be used.

NOTES

SPANISH FISH STEW
(6 Servings)

1	9 oz. pkg. frozen lobster tails
1	lb. shrimp
1	lb. haddock *or* other white fish
2	cloves garlic, minced
¼	cup olive oil
¼	cup brandy
1	med. onion, chopped
½	cup dry white wine
1	1 lb. can tomatoes
1	6 oz. can tomato paste
1	5 oz. jar stuffed olives
1	tsp. salt
½	tsp. sweet basil
¼	tsp. pepper
6	clams

Remove lobster tails from shells and cut into three pieces. Shell the shrimp. Cut the haddock into bite-size pieces. Heat the oil in the pot and cook fish and shellfish with the minced garlic until shellfish turns red, about 5 minutes. Add the brandy, ignite it and shake the pot until the flames die out. Discard the garlic and set the fish and shellfish aside.

In the remaining oil in the pot, sauté the onion until golden, about 5 minutes, stir in the wine, tomatoes, tomato paste, stuffed olives, salt, pepper and sweet basil. Partially cover and simmer for 20 minutes. Add the clams and precooked seafood, cover, and simmer for about 5 minutes or until seafood is heated through.

Serve with crusty bread and a chilled white wine.

Before I give you the impression that all good fish stews originate in the Mediterranean, let me give you the recipe for a stew a friend of mine served at his Malibu Beach house to a most appreciative group of friends. Granted, he had a most effective setting—we sipped our drinks, watching the sun go down and listening to the muted roar of the evening surf—and our appetites were tantalized by the aroma that came drifting from our host's patio kitchen. However, when I tried it in less romantic settings, the dish proved just as successful . . . and I didn't even put *The Surf* on the stereo.

MALIBU FISH STEW
(8-10 Servings)

1	lb. swordfish, skinned and boned
1	lb. halibut, skinned and boned
½	lb. shrimp
1	qt. clams, steamed, shelled *save liquid*
1	2¼ lb. lobster, boiled
6-8	scallops, diced
⅓	cup olive oil
2	med. onions, chopped
1	clove garlic, minced
1	whole stalk celery, diced
4	sprigs parsley
4	ripe med. tomatoes, chopped
1	tsp. crumbled bay leaves
½	tsp. oregano
1-2	tsp. salt *or to taste*
¼	tsp. white pepper *or to taste*
1½-2	cups dry white wine
2	tbs. tomato paste

Cut the cleaned, boned fish into 2″ squares. Shell the shrimp. Steam the clams and save the liquid. Cut the meat from the lobster you boiled earlier in the day, leaving the meat in large chunks. Dice the scallops.

In a large pot heat the oil. Add the chopped onions, garlic and diced stalk of celery, leaves and all, and cook for about 5 minutes until everything is slightly browned. Add the parsley, tomatoes, half of clam liquid, salt, pepper, bay leaves, oregano, white wine and tomato paste. Cover and let simmer for 45 minutes, adding more clam liquid as necessary. Add all the fish and simmer for another 20 minutes.

Serve with a chilled white wine and thick slices of French bread.

MEATS

Socrates once said: "Other men live to eat, while I eat to live."

Years later Emerson stated: "Let the stoics say what they please—we do not eat for the good of living, but because the meat is savory and the appetite is keen."

The Earl of Lytton went even further when he wrote about man:

> He may live without books,—what is
>   knowledge but grieving?
> He may live without hope,—what is
>   hope but deceiving?
> He may live without love,—what is
>   passion but pining?
> But where is the man that can live
>   without dining?

However, the best attitude about dinners might have been expressed by Gertrude Cheney, who back in 1927 at the age of nine philosophized:

> All people are made alike.
> They are made of bones, flesh and dinners.
> Only the dinners are different.

BEEF

In spite of the popularity the steak rightfully enjoys in the United States, nobody has glorified it in words. The only comment on the good old U.S. steak is the rather derogatory one set forth by Edward E. Paramore, Jr.:

> *Oh, tough as a steak was Yukon Jake,*
> *Hard-boiled as a picnic egg.*

Recalling how many juicy steaks I've devoured and served, I certainly cannot share his attitude; I am always ready for steak. However, if I am to serve more than two people I take credence in Byron's lines from *Don Juan:*

> *And nearer as they came, a genial savour*
> *Of certain stews, and roast meats, and pilaus,*
> *Things which in hungry mortals' eyes find favour.*

Mark Twain once said: "Training is everything. The peach was once a bitter almond; cauliflower is nothing but cabbage with a college education."

In the following three recipes I feel the cabbage sneaked through college and graduated with honors.

STUFFED CABBAGE LEAVES
(4 Servings)

8	large white cabbage leaves
2	tsp. olive oil
1	med. onion, chopped
1	15 oz. can tomato sauce
¼	cup dry white wine
1	tsp. salt
¼	tsp. white pepper
¼	tsp. thyme
¼	tsp. crumbled bay leaves
1	lb. ground beef
¼	lb. pork sausage meat
½	cup raw rice
2	tbs. parsley, minced
1	egg
	Parmesan cheese

From a large head of white cabbage pick the eight biggest and best leaves. Trim off hard core and soak in a large bowl in hot, salty water for 5 minutes. Lift out and drain on paper towels.

In a pot heat the oil, add onion and cook until tender and translucent, about 5-10 minutes. Add tomato sauce, wine, thyme, bay leaves, salt and pepper, cover and simmer while you stuff the cabbage leaves.

In the same bowl you used to soak the leaves, mix the beef, sausage, rice, parsley and egg. Season with salt and pepper to taste and divide the meat mixture into eight parts. Place each portion in center of one cabbage leaf, folding the sides over the stuffing, and roll it up from the base of the leaf. Secure each roll with toothpicks or string.

Place the rolls in the simmering sauce, cover, and simmer for another 35 minutes. When ready to serve remove toothpicks or string, sprinkle with Parmesan cheese and serve with sourdough bread and butter.

STUFFED CABBAGE—GREEK STYLE
(4 Servings)

8	large white cabbage leaves
¾	lb. ground beef
¾	lb. ground lamb
2	med. onions, chopped
2	med. tomatoes, chopped
½	cup raw rice
1	tsp. salt
½	tsp. nutmeg
½	tsp. cinnamon
2	tbs. parsley
1	tbs. dried mint
1½	cups water
2	eggs
2	lemons

From a large head of white cabbage pick the eight biggest and best leaves, trim off the hard core and soak in a large bowl in hot, salty water for 5 minutes. Lift out and drain on paper towels.

Discard water from bowl and use for mixing all other ingredients, except the eggs, lemons, and water. Stir mixture well, divide into eight portions and place one in center of each of the cabbage leaves, folding the sides over before starting to roll them up from the base.

Place the rolls in a large pot, cover with water, and weigh them down with a plate. You shouldn't need more than 1½ cups water to cook them in. Simmer, covered, for 1 hour. Fifteen minutes before you're ready to serve, separate your eggs, beat the whites stiff before you add the yolks and then give the mixture another beating. To this, add the juice from the 2 lemons together with a little of the broth from the cabbage leaves. Pour over cabbage leaves, stir lightly to cover all and serve.

If you want to be truly Greek about this dish, you

should use grape leaves, which can be bought in most import grocery stores. But let me warn you; since there's quite a difference in the size of the leaves, it takes a lot longer to stuff the grape leaves, which are finer in texture and have a tart flavor all their own.

NOTES

STUFFED CABBAGE AND SAUERKRAUT
(4-6 Servings)

1	head white cabbage
1½	lbs. ground pork
¾	lb. ground beef
1	egg
¼	cup dry bread crumbs
1	med. onion, chopped
1	tsp. salt
½	tsp. pepper
½	tsp caraway seed
½	tsp. dill weed
1	slice bacon, diced
1	1 lb. can sauerkraut, undrained
3	slices bacon, lightly cooked and drained
2	cups V-8 vegetable juice
1	cup sour cream

Soak the head of cabbage for 10 minutes in a large bowl of boiling water. Drain and carefully separate the leaves, cutting off the hard core or stalks.

Mix together the ground pork and beef with the whole egg, chopped onion, bread crumbs, spices and diced bacon. Divide the mixture among the cabbage leaves, place the meat in the center and fold up the sides before starting to roll them up from the base. Secure with a toothpick.

In the bottom of a large pot spread the canned sauerkraut, arrange the cabbage rolls on top, sprinkle with the lightly cooked, crumbled bacon, pour the vegetable juice over all and simmer, covered, for about 1 hour. Before serving lightly stir in the sour cream and heat through, about 5 minutes.

Serve with chilled beer and slices of rye bread with unsalted butter.

There are two places in Hollywood known for their chili—one is Barney's Beanery, the other Chasen's.

At Barney's Beanery you'll find young struggling artists eating it, prompted by financial reasons; at Chasen's you'll see the famous, long-established stars enjoying it, secure in their knowledge they could have caviar should they so prefer.

The following is as close an approximation of that star-sponsored dish as I've been able to come up with:

CHILI SUPREME
(4 Servings)

2	lbs. ground sirloin
1	tbs. olive oil
2	cloves garlic, minced
1	tsp. MSG
2	onions, chopped
2	green peppers, chopped
½	cup fresh parsley, chopped
¼	lb. butter (1 stick)
⅓	cup chili powder *or to taste*
1	No. 2½ can tomatoes
1-2	No. 303 cans kidney beans
	Salt and pepper *to taste*

Heat the oil in the pot and brown the broken-up meat until it loses its red coloring. Add all other ingredients except the kidney beans, stir well and let simmer for about 1 hour. Check now and then to make sure it doesn't stick to bottom of pot. About 15 minutes before you're ready to serve, add the cans of kidney beans. If you like a moist chili, add liquid from both, otherwise drain before adding the beans.

Serve accompanied by hard-crust rolls, foamy beer and a crisp green salad.

If you prefer a slightly spicier version, try this one:

HOT CHILI
(4 Servings)

1½	lbs. lean ground beef
1	large onion, chopped
2	tbs. butter or margarine
½	cup water
¾	cup dry red wine
1	hot pepper, chopped and seeded
2	med. tomatoes, wedged
2	beef bouillon cubes
1	tbs. chili powder
1	tsp. ground coriander
2	tsp. oregano
1	tsp. salt
½	tsp. pepper
2	No. 303 cans red kidney beans

Melt the butter in the pot and sauté the beef and onion in it until the onion is translucent and the meat, which has been broken with a fork, is brownish in color. Add the water, wine, tomatoes, bouillon cubes and seasoning; bring to a boil, reduce heat and simmer for about 40 minutes, stirring now and then to prevent the meat from sticking to the bottom. In between keep the dish covered. When the mixture is still moist, but not juicy, add the undrained kidney beans and simmer for about 10 minutes or until the beans are thoroughly heated through.

Again serve with a crisp green salad, foamy beer and hard rolls.

If you've grown a little tired of traveling down the more conventional beanery route try this Castilian dish:

CASTILIAN SKILLET DINNER
(3-4 Servings)

1	lb. ground beef
3	tbs. butter or margarine
1	med. onion, chopped
½	cup pitted ripe olives, chopped
½	cup canned garbanzos
½	cup seedless raisins
2	cups V-8 vegetable juice
1	tsp. salt
½	tsp. thyme
½	tsp. marjoram
¼	tsp. pepper

Melt the butter in a large skillet and brown the ground beef in it. Push aside and add the chopped onion, sautéing that for about 5 minutes. Mix together and add the chopped olives together with the garbanzos, raisins, vegetable juice and spices. Simmer gently, covered, until heated through, about 20 minutes. If you feel the mixture is getting a little dry add some water.

Serve with buttered flour tortillas you've heated in a 350° oven for about 10 minutes.

In one of the most unlikely places of all I learned of East Indian cooking. While I was living in Copenhagen, Denmark, I was introduced to a retired Javanese planter who was then running a restaurant on the Copenhagen waterfront. Having picked a name that reeked of English cooking, "The Golden Lamb," he served up the most delicious Javanese dishes, such as the following Kima. Do go to the trouble of getting the individual spices called for rather than substituting curry, for as Voltaire said: "The superfluous is a very necessary thing."

KIMA
(3-4 Servings)

1	med. onion, finely chopped
2	tbs. butter or margarine
½	tsp. salt
½	tsp. ground cumin
½	tsp. turmeric
½	tsp. ginger
1	*dash* black pepper
1	*dash* garlic powder
1	*dash* cayenne
½	tsp. crumbled bay leaves
2	large potatoes, pared and cubed
1	lb. ground beef
1	10 oz. pkg. frozen green peas
1	large tomato, chopped
1	tsp. meat sauce (BVD, Bovaril, etc.)
¼	cup hot water

In a heavy saucepan with a tight-fitting cover, sauté onion in melted butter until golden and translucent. Add salt, cumin, turmeric, ginger, pepper, garlic powder, cayenne and bay leaves. Stir and sauté for 1-2 minutes; now add the cubed potatoes and cook for about 5 minutes or until the edges begin to brown. Make sure you don't scorch the potatoes though.

Add the ground beef, broken up, and brown evenly throughout. Add the peas, tomato, meat sauce and hot water. Stir and cover tightly. Reduce heat and simmer for about 20 minutes or until potatoes are done. Add a little water if necessary, but only enough to keep meat from burning. The dish should be moist, not stewy-juicy.

Serve with hot rolls and follow with fresh fruit and cheese for dessert. Beer goes well with this.

If you've had one of those days where you've been running half an hour to an hour late ever since you started out and still have to get dinner on the table at a reasonable time without calling out for fried chicken, try this quick but savory dish.

NOTES

MEATBALL SKILLET DINNER
(3-4 Servings)

1	egg, slightly beaten
½	cup milk
2	slices white bread, finely diced
½	tsp. nutmeg
¼	tsp. black pepper
½	tsp. celery salt
1	tsp. dry mustard
1	med. onion, grated
1	lb. ground beef
2-3	tbs. butter or margarine
1	can mushroom soup
½	cup milk
¼	cup sherry
1	No. 2 can green beans, drained
	Flour

In a medium-size bowl mix together the egg, ½ cup of milk and finely diced bread; add all the spices, the grated onion and the meat. Mix well and shape into 1" balls. Dust with flour.

In a pot or deep skillet melt the butter and brown the meatballs. When they are well done on all sides remove them to a platter and keep warm. Into the skillet stir the undiluted mushroom soup, the other ½ cup milk and the sherry; let the mixture simmer for 2-3 minutes before adding the meatballs and green beans. Simmer until everything is heated through, about 5-10 minutes.

Serve with rolls and marinated tomato slices.

If you aren't quite as pressed for time and feel a little more fanciful and exotic, you might want to try this colorful and different way of serving meatballs.

ORANGE MEATBALLS
(4 Servings)

1	lb. ground beef
1	med. onion, grated
½	tsp. salt
¼	tsp. pepper
¼	tsp. cinnamon
4-6	tbs. butter or margarine
2	tbs. butter or margarine
3	cups finely chopped raw spinach
1	cup finely chopped fresh parsley
1	cup water
1	beef bouillon cube
1	cup orange juice
¼	cup lemon juice
1	tbs. flour
¼	cup pine nuts, crisped
	Chinese noodles

Mix together the ground beef, grated onion, salt, pepper and cinnamon and shape into tiny balls. In bottom of pot or deep skillet heat 4-6 tbs. butter and brown meatballs well on all sides. Remove and keep warm. This is easily done by wrapping them in aluminum foil and sticking them into the broiler section of the stove with just the pilot light on. Add the 2 remaining tbs. of butter to the pot and when melted stir in the chopped spinach and parsley. Cook for about 10 minutes, stirring frequently.

Return the meatballs to the pot, add the water and the bouillon cube and let the whole thing simmer for about 15 minutes. Combine the orange and lemon juices with the flour, stir into pot and let simmer for another 20 minutes. Just before serving with Chinese noodles, sprinkle the pine nuts, which have been crisped in the oven, over the whole dish. A chilled bottle of vin rosé goes very nicely with this.

Some of my puritan friends—gastronomically speaking —feel that my version of beef stroganoff is, if not sacrilegious, at least not kosher. However, since others prefer it to the more accepted version, I include it; you can be the judge.

NOTES

BEEF STROGANOFF A LA HANNAH
(4 Servings)

1½   lbs. top sirloin, cut in ½" strips
2-3   tbs. butter or margarine
2-3   med. onions, sliced
½   tsp. salt
¼   tsp. pepper
1   8 oz. can tomato sauce
1   can dry red wine
2-3   med. tomatoes, in wedges
2   beef bouillon cubes
½   tsp. thyme
12   large, fresh mushrooms, washed
    and quartered
1   small container commercial sour cream
    Rice Krispies

In a deep skillet or medium-size pot melt the butter or margarine and sauté the sliced onion for about 5-10 minutes until translucent and limp. Push aside and brown the meat strips on both sides. Mix the meat and the onions, sprinkle with salt, pepper and thyme and pour over this equal amounts of tomato sauce and dry red wine; stir in the tomato wedges and bouillon cubes, cover and simmer over low heat for about 30 minutes. Now add the fresh mushrooms and simmer for another 15 minutes. Two-three minutes before you're ready to serve, stir in the sour cream and let it heat through, but not boil.

If you wonder what the Rice Krispies are for, I serve my Beef Stroganoff over them rather than noodles or rice. Don't be alarmed over it—try it, once, please, and you'll be surprised how good it is. But do make sure it's the regular kind of Rice Krispies, not the sugar-frosted sort. If you're met by doubting Thomases just quote Brillat-Savarin: "The discovery of a new dish does more for the happiness of man than the discovery of a star."

Want to bring the Orient to your house? Try this Americanized version of the popular Japanese dish, su-kiyaki.

If you have an electric skillet, you can cook it right in front of your sake-sipping guests; if not, a regular skillet on top of the stove will do, but don't experiment with a chafing dish. I did, and it didn't work.

Either way take care of your slicing before you start the actual cooking, which only takes about 25 minutes.

NOTES

SUKIYAKI—OCCIDENTAL STYLE
(3-4 Servings)

2	tbs. olive oil
1	Bermuda onion, sliced
6	scallions, cut in 1" pieces
3	whole stalks celery, sliced in ½" pieces
8	mushrooms, cleaned and sliced
1	10 oz. pkg. frozen green beans
1	1 lb. can bean sprouts
⅔	cup consomme
⅓	cup soy sauce
⅓	cup sherry
2	tbs. lemon juice
2	tbs. sugar
1	lb. flank steak, thinly sliced
	Chinese noodles

Prepare all the vegetables and meat before you heat the oil in a large skillet. Add the sliced onion and scallion pieces and brown lightly. Add the sliced celery, the mushrooms, frozen green beans and drained bean sprouts. Stir in all the liquids and the sugar and cook for about 10 minutes, stirring occasionally.

Push the vegetables aside, add the thinly slivered meat and continue cooking until the meat loses its color and is heated through.

Serve over Chinese noodles and accompany with sake served in delicate china cups.

I recommend the following two "he-man" recipes to any woman who's trying to get something special out of the man in her life. Both can be started the day before or in the morning and finished at the time appropriate for executing the *coup de grâce*.

BRAISED SHORT RIBS AND CHICK PEAS
(4-6 Servings)

3	lbs. short ribs, in pairs or threesomes
2	tsp. salt
½	tsp. pepper
1	cup dry red wine
1	cup water
2	beef bouillon cubes
½	tsp. oregano
½	tsp. dried mint
1	large onion, chopped
2	large stalks celery with leaves, chopped
3	med. carrots, 1″ pieces
1	lb. can chick peas, drained

In a Dutch oven or other large pot, brown the ribs on all sides. Pour off any excess fat and sprinkle them with salt and pepper. Add the wine, water, bouillon cubes, oregano and mint. Bring to a boil, reduce heat and simmer for 1 hour and 30 minutes. Add the onion, celery and carrots, continue simmering for another 20 minutes, then stir in the chick peas. Heat about 10 minutes and serve accompanied by foamy beer or a dry red wine.

If you start the dish ahead of time you should stop before adding the vegetables to prevent them from going soggy.

SHORT RIBS EXTRAORDINAIRE
(4-6 Servings)

2-3	tbs. butter or margarine
3	lbs. short ribs, English cut, in twos or threes
2	tsp. salt
¼	tsp. pepper
½	tsp. crumbled bay leaves
½	tsp. caraway seed
¾	cup beer
1-2	beef bouillon cubes
6-8	small white onions
4	carrots, halved
½	lb. rutabagas, pared and cubed
1	10 oz. pkg. frozen peas
½	cup water

Melt the butter in bottom of ovenproof pot and brown the ribs over medium heat, dusted with flour if you like. When well browned on both sides, and this will take about 25 minutes, add the salt and pepper together with the herbs, beer and bouillon cubes. Cover and bake at 350° for about 1 hour and 30 minutes. Add the peeled, white onions, the pared and halved carrots, the diced rutabagas and the peas together with the ½ cup of water and continue baking for another 45 minutes . . . or 1 hour, should he want another martini.

Serve with sourdough bread, and have plenty of beer on hand in the refrigerator, as it goes very smoothly with this dish. Again, if you start ahead of time, stop before you add the vegetables and pick up from there 1 hour before you want to serve.

"When a man is invited to dinner he's disappointed not to get something good," Samuel Johnson once said.

If you want to live up to those words you can safely serve either of the two following pot roasts. One recipe I picked up in France, the other is an updated version of grandmother's favorite recipe. Both are worth trying and both can be started one day and finished the next, if that fits your schedule better . . . pot roasts do have to cook for a rather long time.

NOTES

FRENCH POT ROAST
(6 Servings)

¼	cup bacon drippings
4-5	lbs. rump roast
2½	cups dry red wine
¼	cup water
2	beef bouillon cubes
1	tbs. hot pepper sauce
½	tsp. nutmeg
½	tsp. thyme
½	tsp. crumbled bay leaves
¼	tsp. dried tarragon
6	celery tops, 1½″ pieces
12	small carrots, scraped
12	small white onions, peeled
½	lbs. fresh mushrooms, washed and quartered

Heat the bacon drippings in a large kettle and brown the whole piece of meat well on all sides. This takes about 15-20 minutes. Pour off excess drippings before adding the wine, water, bouillon cubes, pepper sauce, nutmeg, thyme, bay leaves, tarragon and celery tops. Cover the pot with a tight fitting lid and let simmer for about 3 hours, turning the meat occasionally.

Skim off excess fat and add the carrots and onions, letting them simmer under cover for another 30 minutes before adding the mushrooms. After 15 minutes more of simmering you're ready to serve.

Pick the meat out of the pot and carve on a board or platter, serving the vegetables right out of the pot. Have some good sourdough bread on hand for the gravy; and if you feel in the mood, a bottle of Burgundy goes nicely with this.

GRANDMAMA'S FRUITY POT ROAST
(6 Servings)

4	**lbs. beef pot roast**
	Seasoned meat tenderizer
1-2	**tbs. butter or margarine**
1	**large onion, sliced**
½	**tsp. cinnamon**
3	**tbs. brown sugar**
¼	**cup honey**
¼	**cup water**
¾	**cup dried prunes, pitted**
¾	**cup dried apricots**
1	**can light beer**
½	**tsp. ginger**
6	**med. potatoes, pared and sliced**

With a fork, pierce the roast generously on all sides and sprinkle with meat tenderizer all over according to the labeled directions. Do this at least 1 hour before you start cooking. In a Dutch oven heat the butter and brown the meat evenly on all sides. This will take you about 20-25 minutes. Add the large sliced onion, keeping your eye on the meat as you let the onion slices get slightly brown. Now add the cinnamon, brown sugar, honey and water, mixing well. Cover tightly and simmer over low heat for about 1 hour and 45 minutes.

Meanwhile soak the dried fruits in the beer in a medium-size bowl, adding the ginger to the liquid. When the simmering time is up, arrange the sliced potatoes and soaked fruits in alternate layers around the roast, pouring any excess liquid over it all. Cover tightly again and simmer for an additional 30 minutes or until the potatoes are done.

Carve the meat on a platter or board and serve the rest right out of the pot.

Since I do on occasion give in to my masochistic traits and serve a roast with all the trimmings, I, like everybody else, have been faced with how to turn the uneven and not-too-exciting leftovers into a tasty meal.

Below are two ways not too common—one I picked up in Denmark, the other takes its inspiration from the Orient. Both have the distinct advantage that you don't immediately think "leftovers" at the sight of them.

NOTES

DANISH FARMER'S POT
(4 Servings)

2-3	cups leftover beef
2-3	med. potatoes, pared and sliced
2-3	celeriacs, pared and cubed or diced
3-4	carrots, cubed
2	med. onions, sliced
4	tbs. butter or margarine
1	8 oz. can tomato sauce
1	can beer
1	tsp. fennel seed
1-2	tsp. salt
¼	tsp. black pepper
2	large tomatoes, quartered

In a pot, melt the butter and sauté the diced celeriac with the onion for about 10 minutes. If the onion gets a little brown along the edges, it's okay. Add the carrots and potatoes, stir and sprinkle with salt, pepper and fennel seed before stirring in the tomato sauce and beer. Cover and simmer for about 15 minutes. Now add the leftover meat which has been cut in strips or shreds, and continue simmering for another 20-30 minutes. During the last 10 minutes, stir in the quartered tomatoes. If you find the dish a little too juicy, let it simmer without a cover during the last 15 minutes.

Serve with pumpernickel and beer and make sure you have a bottle of Worcestershire sauce on the table as well.

CHINESE SKILLET BEEF
(4 Servings)

2	tbs. peanut or olive oil
1	med. head cauliflower, in flowerettes
¼	cup water
1	can undiluted consomme
1½	tbs. cornstarch
2	tbs. soy sauce
2	tbs. lemon juice
2	scallions, diced
2	cups leftover beef, in strips
1	10 oz. pkg. frozen peas
1	tsp. salt.
	Chinese noodles

Heat the oil in a deep skillet and sauté the broken cauliflower for about 3 minutes, stirring constantly, making sure it doesn't brown. Reduce the heat, add water, cover and let steam for 2-3 minutes or until tender-crisp.

Mix together the consomme, cornstarch, soy sauce, lemon juice and finely diced scallions, stir well and pour over cauliflower. Add the leftover meat cut into thin strips, the peas and salt, giving it a good stir. Cook over medium heat until steaming hot and sauce is thickened. Serve with Chinese noodles.

When asked about life, W. C. Handy, the famed composer of "The St. Louis Blues," once said: "Life is something like my trumpet. If you don't put anything in it you don't get anything out. And that's the truth."

Truer and simpler words were never spoken, and the same theory could be applied to food. The following rec-

ipes use beef stew meat as their base, but all are enhanced by the subtle ingredients added.

As Robert Herrick wrote:

'Tis not the food, but the content,
That makes the table's merriment.

NOTES

GOULASH EXTRAORDINAIRE
(4-6 Servings)

2	tbs. butter or margarine
2	lbs. beef stew meat
3	med. onions, chopped
4	tsp. paprika
1	large tomato, chopped
½	tsp. marjoram
¼	tsp. caraway seed
1-2	tsp. salt
¼	tsp. black pepper
½	tsp. bay leaves, crumbled
1½	lbs. smoked ham, in large cubes
¾	cup dry red wine
¾	cup water
1	bouillon cube
4	large potatoes, peeled and cut in eighths
½	cup commercial sour cream
3	hard-boiled eggs, sliced

In a large kettle or Dutch oven melt the butter. Add beef and brown slowly but well on all sides, stirring it with a wooden spoon to prevent scorching. Add onions and continue cooking them slowly until they are translucent. Add the paprika and stir until well blended. Add tomato and ham cubes, sprinkle with the herbs, spices and bouillon cube, and into this pour half the wine and water. Cover and cook slowly for 2 hours, making sure it never boils and adding more wine and water as needed. After 2 hours add the potatoes and cook slowly for another 30 minutes or until the potatoes are done.

Just before serving, stir in the sour cream and top the whole thing with slices of hard-boiled eggs, arranged in whatever pattern is your fancy.

Serve with slices of rye bread, a crisp green salad and a bottle of Burgundy.

The following is the traditional Viennese recipe, a little less fanciful and time-consuming, but as tasty as anything that comes out of Vienna.

NOTES

VIENNESE BEEF GOULASH
(4-6 Servings)

1½	lbs. beef stew meat
2	med. onions, chopped
4	tbs. butter or margarine
1-2	tsp. caraway seed
½	tsp. marjoram
2	cloves garlic, minced
1	can light beer
1	cup water
1-2	tsp. salt
6	med. potatoes, pared and quartered
3	tbs. paprika
4	tbs. tomato catsup
3	hard-boiled eggs, sliced
	Sour cream

Melt the butter in a large pot and sauté the chopped onion in it for about 5 minutes or until translucent. Add the beef, herbs and spices, beer and water. Stir, bring to a boil, reduce heat and simmer for 45 minutes to 1 hour, or until meat is semi-tender to a fork. Add the quartered potatoes and simmer for another 30 minutes or until potatoes are done. During the last 10 minutes add the paprika mixed into the tomato catsup, giving everything a good stir.

Serve with slices of hard-boiled eggs on top and have sour cream, slices of rye bread and foamy beer on hand.

The following recipe for Indian Curry comes from my retired planter friend in Copenhagen. He had brought with him from Java all sorts of exotic condiments such as salty dried shark fins, dried roots, etc., which I haven't been able to track down . . . but the recipe stands on its own without them as well.

If you're a purist at heart, as was he, and want to serve
your rice separately, you can of course do so . . . you're
doing the dishes. In that case don't add the water, bouillon
cubes and rice to the meat mixture. You should, however,
still allow for the meat to cook 1 hour and 30 minutes.

NOTES

INDIAN BEEF CURRY
(4 Servings)

¼	cup butter or margarine
2	large onions, sliced
2	cloves garlic, minced
1	tbs. powdered coriander
1	tsp. powdered turmeric
½	tsp. ground cumin
½	tsp. ground ginger
¼	tsp. dry mustard
¼	tsp. powdered cardamon
1-2	tsp. salt
2	tbs. wine vinegar
2	large tomatoes, wedged
2	lbs. beef stew or chuck, cubed
1½	cups water
1	cup rice
1	beef bouillon cube

Melt the butter in a heavy saucepan or pot. Sauté the onion and garlic for about 10 minutes. Mix all the spices, including the salt, with the vinegar and pour over onion mixture. Simmer for about 2-3 minutes. Add the beef and tomatoes to the mixture, stir, cover and simmer for about 1 hour over low heat. Now add the water, bouillon cube and rice, stir well and cover, letting everything simmer for another 30 minutes, giving the mixture a stir after the first 15 minutes to make the rice nice and fluffy.

Serve with hard rolls and condiments such as salted peanuts, diced cucumber, chopped hard-boiled eggs, diced pimento, etc. A glass of beer also goes nicely with this.

As you will note from the name of the following dish, its appearance varies from that of a regular stew.

It should be accompanied by buttered pumpernickel and beer, the Danes' national drink. I'm sure they're still a little unhappy it wasn't one of their poets who immortalized the merits of this noble drink but rather the English poet, John Gay, who in his "A Ballad on Ale" says:

> *Give me a bumper, fill it up:*
> *See how it sparkles in the cup;*
> *O how shall I regale!*
> *Can any taste this drink divine,*
> *And then compare rum, brandy, wine*
> *Or aught, with nappy Ale!*

DANISH SAILOR'S MASH
(4 Servings)

8	slices bacon
2	lbs. beef stew
2	onions, sliced
2	large leeks, ½″ pieces
½	tsp. caraway seed
1	tsp. dill weed
¼	tsp. crumbled bay leaves
½	tsp. thyme
6	whole peppercorns
1-2	tsp. salt
2	bouillon cubes
2	cups water
4	med. potatoes, sliced
1	med. celeriac, sliced
4	carrots, 1″ pieces
¼	tsp. fennel seed

Brown the bacon in a pot, remove and drain on a paper towel. Sauté the chopped onion and leeks in the remaining drippings over low heat for about 10 minutes. Add the meat, stir well, and sprinkle with herbs (except fennel seed) and spices before adding the bouillon cubes and water. Bring to a boil, reduce heat and let simmer for 1 hour and 15 minutes. Now add potatoes, celeriac, carrots and fennel seed and continue simmering for another 45 minutes, by which time it will have the consistency of lumpy mashed potatoes, guaranteeing any seafaring man that his dinner will stay on the plate.

As I said earlier, serve with buttered pumpernickel and beer and have a bottle of Worcestershire on hand for those who might like that.

According to the unabridged dictionary a *ragout* is a highly seasoned stew of meat or fish, with or without vegetables, whereas a *stew* is a preparation of meat, fish or other food cooked by stewing, especially a mixture of meat and vegetables. These definitions, to me at least, help more to prove the abundance of words in the English language than setting forth the difference between the two dishes involved . . . so here follows the Traditional Beef Ragout, unless you were first introduced to it as the Traditional Beef Stew.

TRADITIONAL BEEF RAGOUT
(6-8 Servings)

3	lbs. lean beef stew
3	tbs. olive oil
3	tbs. flour
2	cups dry red wine
1	cup water
1	clove garlic, crushed
1	tsp. crumbled bay leaves
1-2	tsp. salt
½	tsp. pepper
½	tsp. dried thyme
1	tbs. parsley flakes
12	small carrots, scraped
12	small white onions, peeled
6-8	med. potatoes, pared and halved
1	10 oz. pkg. frozen green peas
6	small turnips, pared and halved

In a heavy pot or Dutch oven heat the oil and brown the beef cubes well on all sides. Sprinkle in the flour, stir and cook until flour is lightly browned. Stir in wine and water, together with the crushed garlic, crumbled bay leaves, salt, pepper, thyme and parsley. Cover tightly, bring to a boil, then reduce heat and let simmer until meat is almost tender, about 1 hour.

While the beef is cooking, prepare the vegetables. After the hour is up add all the vegetables except the frozen peas. Stir well and continue simmering under cover for another 30-45 minutes. When the turnips and potatoes are almost tender, add the thawed-out peas and simmer for an additional 15 minutes. Adjust for salt and serve with garlic bread and a bottle of red wine.

The Beef Bourguignon that follows takes a little time to prepare, so don't plan to rush home from the office and fix it. Take your own good time on a Saturday or Sunday and serve it to appreciative, special guests, keeping in mind the advice the Earl of Chesterfield gave his son: "Whatever is worth doing, is worth doing well."

NOTES

BEEF BOURGUIGNON
(4 Servings)

2	lbs. beef stew
1	cup dry red wine
2	tbs. olive oil
1	large onion, sliced
½	tsp. thyme
1	tbs. parsley flakes
1	tsp. bay leaves, crumbled
¼	tsp. pepper
2	thick slices bacon, diced
1	tbs. olive oil
6	small white onions, peeled
8	large mushrooms, washed and quartered
2	tbs. flour
2	scallions, 1″ pieces
1	tsp. salt *or to taste*
½	cup brandy
1	tsp. dried orange peel
¾	cup water
1	bouillon cube
4	med. potatoes, pared and quartered

In the morning—or at least 3 hours before you plan to
start cooking—marinate the meat in the red wine to which
you've added the 2 tbs. olive oil, the sliced onion, thyme,
parsley, crumbled bay leaves and pepper.

In a heavy pot or Dutch oven heat the 1 tbs. of oil,
add the diced bacon and let it slowly brown. Remove
bacon pieces and drain on paper towel. Add the white
onions to the pot and let them glaze evenly, sautéing them
for about 5-10 minutes. Remove and put aside. Now do
the same thing with the mushrooms: sauté and put aside.
Drain the meat of its marinade, saving the marinade. Wipe
the meat pieces dry in paper toweling and brown them in

the pot, a few pieces at the time. When all the meat is browned, sprinkle with flour and stir until all the flour is absorbed.

Pour the brandy in, scrape the sides of any little bits that may be clinging and let brandy simmer until it's almost evaporated. Now add the marinade to the pot; you can strain it if you want to, but I don't. Stir in the water, bouillon cube, scallions and dried orange peel. Bring to a boil, reduce heat and let simmer for about 2 hours. Add the bacon, white onions, quartered potatoes and mushrooms which had been sautéed earlier and simmer for another 40 minutes under cover. If you think the dish is getting a little too dry add a little more wine and water, but then also another bouillon cube.

Serve with hard rolls and a bottle of good red wine followed by a cheese and fruit tray.

Whether it's the annual plum pudding, the crepes suzette you fix on rare occasions, or the special shish kebab you have with your favorite date at your very own Armenian restaurant, there's something festive about a flaming dish. So when you go to the trouble of fixing the following Beef Flambé, make sure the occasion fits the dish.

BEEF FLAMBE ROUGE
(4-6 Servings)

2	lbs. sirloin tip, cubed or same amount beef stew
4	slices bacon
½	tsp. crumbled bay leaves
1	tsp. salt
1	tsp. oregano
½	tsp. MSG
½	tsp. freshly ground pepper
¼	cup red wine vinegar
3	whole cloves
½	cup dry red wine
½	cup consomme *or*
½	cup water and 1 bouillon cube
2	tbs. flour
12	small white onions, peeled
1	large green pepper, in strips
½	lb. fresh mushrooms, washed and sliced
½	box cherry tomatoes
¼	cup brandy

If you don't mind the difference in price do use sirloin tip for this dish, but stew meat will do nicely.

Fry the bacon to a crisp in a Dutch oven, remove and drain on paper towels. Pour all but 2 tbs. of bacon drippings into your grease container. In the remaining 2 tbs. of bacon drippings, slowly brown the meat well, cut into 1½" cubes. Add the peeled white onions, the crumbled bay leaves, cloves, salt, pepper, oregano, MSG, vinegar, wine and consomme; give it a good stir, bring to a boil before reducing heat to let it simmer for 1 hour under cover. Now add the green pepper, cut into fairly thin strips, together with the sliced mushrooms and continue

simmering for another 15 minutes. Add the cherry tomatoes, cut in halves and, if you like a thicker gravy, the 2
tbs. of flour stirred into a little water. Continue simmering
for another 5 minutes or so.

Bring the pot to the table, pour the warmed brandy over
the dish, ignite the brandy and gently stir it into the mixture. When the flames have died down you're ready to
serve. Have some good rolls on hand together with a bottle
of Burgundy.

In the following recipe, please don't substitute the beer
called for with water. The beer does something very special
to its flavor. In the words of Harry Leon Wilson:

> *While beer brings gladness, don't forget*
> *That water only makes you wet.*

In this case the beer adds a happy note to the stew.

BEERY BEEF STEW
(4-6 Servings)

¼	cup flour
1	tsp. salt
½	tsp. pepper
2	lbs. stew meat, 1" cubes
½	cup olive oil
2	lbs. onions, peeled and sliced
1	clove garlic, crushed
1	giant-size can beer
1	tbs. soy sauce
1	tbs. Worcestershire sauce
1	tbs. steak sauce
½	tsp. crumbled bay leaves
1	tsp. dried thyme
2	lbs. potatoes. pared and quartered
4	med. carrots, in chunks
	Boiling water
	Parsley

Coat the cubed meat in the flour which has been mixed with salt and pepper; set aside.

In a large pot heat ¼ cup of the olive oil and sauté the onion and garlic until tender, about 5 minutes. Remove onion from the pot, add the remaining oil, heat, and add the floured meat, browning it well on all sides. Return the onion-garlic mixture along with the beer, the three sauces and herbs. Mix well, bring mixture to a boil, reduce heat, cover and simmer for 1 hour and 30 minutes. Add the pared, quartered potatoes to the stew with just enough boiling water to make enough juice for them to cook in. After about 15 minutes, add the carrots. In another 20 minutes or so, when the potatoes are tender, you're ready to serve, sprinkling some parsley on top just before carrying the pot to the table.

Serve with a crisp green salad and hard rolls.

Did you have one of those mornings when you took sharp issue with your husband's sudden change on politics, forgetting momentarily Tristan Bernard's advice: "Men are always sincere. They change sincerities, that's all"?

If you have cooled down and want to break the armed neutrality that might have settled over your household, there's hardly any better way than serving the following stew with dumplings.

NOTES

CARAWAY BEEF STEW WITH DUMPLINGS
(4 Servings)

2	lbs. beef stew meat
2-3	tbs. olive oil
1	cup dry red wine
1	cup water
2	beef bouillon cubes
1	tsp. thyme
½	tsp. caraway seed
¼	tsp. black pepper
4-6	carrots, sliced
6	small white onions, peeled
2	green peppers, in strips
2	turnips, peeled and cubed

DUMPLINGS

¾	cup milk
½	tsp. seasoned salt
½	tsp. caraway seed
2	cups Bisquick

Brown the stew meat in hot oil in large pot. Add the wine, water, bouillon cubes and herbs to the well-browned meat, stir and bring to a boil before you reduce the heat. Cover and simmer for 30 minutes. Add the onions and turnips and continue simmering, covered, for another 30 minutes, then add the green peppers and carrots. In another 30 minutes the stew is ready.

While the stew is simmering let the milk absorb the flavor of the seasoned salt and caraway seed. About 15 minutes before you're ready to serve, stir the flavored milk into the Bisquick, to make a batter and drop from a teaspoon into the stew . . . after you have pushed the meat into the center with a wooden spoon. Let the dumplings simmer, covered, for about 10 minutes in the juicy edges, and you're ready to serve.

Sliced cucumbers and tomatoes in an oil and vinegar dressing go very well with this as does a bottle of red wine.

If you have teen-agers in your family whose preference goes toward hamburgers and chili con carne, you'll find that the next recipe will meet with their whole-hearted approval, sending them merrily on their way toward a more sophisticated choice of entrees.

CHILI BEEF STEW
(4-6 Servings)

3	lbs. beef stew meat
½	cup flour
3	tsp. salt
¼	tsp. pepper
2	tsp. chili powder
½	tsp. ground coriander
¼	cup olive oil
1	large onion, minced
1	tsp. caraway seed
1	tsp. marjoram
1	cup dry red wine
½	cup water
1	beef bouillon cube
6-8	small white onions, peeled
4-5	carrots, in chunks
3	large tomatoes, quartered

Combine the flour, salt, pepper, chili powder and ground coriander in a paper bag and dredge the cubed meat in this before browning it well on all sides in hot oil. Add any remaining flour to the browned meat together with the minced onion, caraway seed, marjoram, water, wine and bouillon cube. Bring to a boil, reduce heat and simmer for 1 hour and 30 minutes.

Add the white onions, carrots and tomatoes and continue simmering for another 45 minutes, stirring once or twice, after you've peeked under the cover to see if it's juicy enough.

Serve with flour tortillas, heated in a low oven and buttered at the table.

Now if you're a working girl but still want to impress somebody special with your cooking during the week, the following is the recipe for it.

You can start it the evening before—or in the morning if you're one of those people who likes to allow himself a lot of time before leaving for the office. You stop the cooking before adding the artichokes. All you have to do in the evening is attend to it once or twice before serving, leaving you ample time to find out if the average man is more interested in a woman who is interested in him than he is in a woman—any woman—with beautiful legs. It was Marlene Dietrich who said that, and she certainly should know whereof she speaks.

ELEGANT BEEF STEW
(4 Servings)

1½	lbs. lean stew beef
¼	cup flour
1	tsp. salt
½	tsp. pepper
2	tbs. olive oil
2	8 oz. cans tomato sauce
½	cup red wine
½	cup water
2	beef bouillon cubes
½	tsp. dill weed
½	tsp. sweet basil
8	small white onions, peeled
1	10 oz. pkg. frozen artichoke hearts
8	large mushrooms, washed and quartered

Mix the flour, salt and pepper in a bag and shake the cubed meat in this, drenching the individual pieces well. In a pot heat the oil and brown the meat well on all sides. Stir in the peeled white onions, sprinkle with dill and sweet basil, tuck the bouillon cubes in and pour the tomato sauce, wine and water over everything. Give it a good stir, bring to a boil, reduce heat and let simmer under cover for 1 hour and 15 minutes. Add the artichoke hearts and simmer for another 15 minutes before you add the mushrooms. Stir and continue simmering under cover for another 15-20 minutes.

Serve with thin breadsticks and a bottle of red wine, followed by your own favorite dessert or some good imported chocolate with your after-dinner coffee.

The following is a less expensive but very good stew that readily brings to mind the words of Sidney Smith:

> *Serenely full, the epicure would say,*
> *Fate cannot harm me, I have dined today.*

PINK BEEF STEW
(4 Servings)

2	tbs. flour
½	tsp. salt
¼	tsp. pepper
1	lb. beef stew meat
2	tbs. butter or margarine
1	can cream of tomato soup
½	cup dry red wine
½	cup water
1	beef bouillon cube
3	carrots, scraped, 1″ pieces
1	tbs. parsley flakes
1	tsp. Worcestershire sauce
⅛	tsp. caraway seed
1½	cups shredded white cabbage

Drench the cubed meat in flour mixed with salt and pepper and brown it well on all sides in melted butter. Add the tomato soup, wine, water and bouillon cube, stir and bring to a boil; cover and let simmer for 1 hour and 15 minutes. Now add the carrots, parsley, Worcestershire sauce, shredded cabbage and caraway seed, stirring well before you continue simmering under cover for another 45 minutes.

The original recipe for the following stew called for squirrel, but I have neither the inclination nor the butcher for that and will readily accept the substitute beef and chicken in this more modern version.

BRUNSWICK STEW
(6 Servings)

5	lbs. chicken, cut into serving pieces
1	lb. beef stew meat, cubed
6	cups water
3	beef bouillon cubes
2	12 oz. cans beer
3	large onions, chopped
1-2	tsp. salt
½	tsp. marjoram
½	tsp. sweet basil
½	tsp. thyme
1	10 oz. pkg. frozen lima beans
1	10 oz. pkg. frozen okra
3	med. potatoes, pared and cubed
2	tbs. tomato catsup
2	stalks celery, 1″ pieces
2	tomatoes, wedged
1	No. 2 can whole kernel corn, drained
4	tbs. butter
4	tbs. sugar
2	tbs. vinegar

Place the pieces of chicken in a large pot or kettle together with the cubed beef and onions. Sprinkle with salt and herbs, tuck in the bouillon cubes and pour the beer and water over all. Cook over low heat for 1 hour and 30 minutes. Spoon out chicken pieces and beef and set aside. Now add the lima beans, okra, potatoes, catsup, celery, tomatoes, drained corn and butter to the stock. Bring to a boil, reduce heat, and simmer for another 30 minutes while you pull the meat off the chicken pieces. After 30 minutes return the two meats to the pot and cook, uncovered, until most of the liquid has evaporated. Stir in sugar and vinegar 5 minutes before you are ready to serve.

Here again, I would recommend soup bowls rather than regular dinner plates, and lots of bread with which to sop up the juices. It really can be done quite daintily with a fork, and it's mighty tasty!

The following is a delicious stew that will serve you very well at a party. Again you can start it the day before, stopping after you've added the onions and carrots. The next day you bring it back to simmering, add mushrooms and artichokes and proceed as directed.

The end result lives up to the statement Oscar Wilde once made: "After a good dinner, one can forgive anybody, even one's own relations."

PARTY STEW
(6-8 Servings)

2	lbs. beef stew, cubed
1	lb. lean lamb, cubed
1	lb. lean veal, in strips
1/3	cup olive oil
2	large onions, sliced
1/2	tsp. thyme
1/2	tsp. oregano
1	tbs. salt
2	tbs. parsley flakes
1	tbs. butter
1	cup water
1	cup dry red wine
1	pkg. frozen artichoke hearts
1	beef bouillon cube
8-10	small white onions, peeled
6-8	carrots, in chunks
3/4	lb. fresh mushrooms, washed and quartered
1	cup red wine
4	large tomatoes, quartered
3/4	cup wild and long grain rice
1/2	tsp. freshly ground black pepper

In a large pot, heat the oil and brown all the meats well on all sides. Push meats aside, or place them on a platter while you sauté the onion slices, allowing them to get lightly brown. Mix meats and onions, sprinkle with thyme, oregano, salt and parsley flakes; dot with butter, tuck in bouillon cube and pour wine and water over it all. Bring to a boil, reduce heat and let simmer for 1 hour and 30 minutes.

Now add the white onions, carrots, mushrooms, frozen artichokes and quartered tomatoes. Continue simmering for another 15 minutes before you add the mixed rice together with the last cup of wine. Stir well, cover, and simmer for another 30 minutes, giving the stew a good stir after 15. If you think the pot is getting too juicy, leave the cover off during the last 10-15 minutes.

Serve with a crisp lettuce and cucumber salad and one or two of those prebaked frozen loaves of breads you can get at the grocery store. It goes without saying that this deserves a really good bottle of Burgundy.

To fix the following recipe, you had better figure on being in the house—although not necessarily in the kitchen—the whole afternoon. But believe me, it's an afternoon well spent. It's the kind of meal that would forever prevent your fellow from heeding the advice Ambrose Bierce once gave a friend: "You are not permitted to kill a woman who has wronged you, but nothing forbids you to reflect that she is growing older every minute. You are avenged 1,440 times a day."

POT AU FEU
(6-8 Servings)

3	qts. water
8	1″ marrow bones
2	lbs. beef stew meat, cubed
2	lbs. chicken, in serving pieces
4	bratwursts, in 1-2″ pieces
1	onion, peeled, studded with 2 cloves
2	leeks, in 1″ pieces
3	carrots, in 1″ pieces
1	large turnip, pared and quartered
2	stalks celery, 2″ pieces
½	head cabbage, wedged
½	tsp. crumbled bay leaves
1	tbs. parsley flakes
½	tsp. thyme
1-2	tsp. salt
½	tsp. pepper

Tie the marrow bones into a piece of cheesecloth and place in a large kettle: pour over just enough water to cover, bring to a boil, reduce heat and simmer for 2 hours. Pull out the cheesecloth sack, saving the bones. Add 3 quarts of water to broth in kettle and put in the beef stew meat, the chicken pieces and the bratwursts. Bring to a boil, reduce heat, cover and simmer for 40 minutes. Add the clove-studded onion, the leeks, carrots and cabbage wedges, together with the turnip, celery, herbs and salt and pepper. Partially cover the pot and simmer for another 1 hour and 15 minutes.

After 30 minutes of this, spoon out the chicken pieces. When cool enough to handle, pull the meat off the bones and keep it warm. Return the meat to the pot about 10 minutes before cooking time is up. During the last 5 minutes, submerge the marrow bones still tied up in the cheesecloth.

When you're ready to serve, place a marrow bone in each soup plate or bowl and ladle the contents of the pot over this. Have plenty of crusty warm bread and chilled vin rosé on hand for this feast.

NOTES

CHICKEN

An anonymous writer once commented on the merits of the egg-laying process in a verse that could be right out of the works of *Laugh-In's* Henry Gibson:

> *The codfish lays ten thousand eggs,*
> *The homely hen lays one.*
> *The codfish never cackles*
> *To tell you what she's done.*
> *And so we scorn the codfish*
> *While the homely hen we prize,*
> *Which only goes to show you*
> *That it pays to advertise.*

Maybe if the hen had stopped to think of the dangers involved in calling attention to herself and her products, she would have altered the menu for many a Sunday supper. Certainly no political slogan was ever taken more seriously than Henry the Fourth's: "I want there to be no peasant in my realm so poor that he will not have a chicken in his pot every Sunday."

However, whether it was the hen's cackling or the flavor of the chicken's meat that prompted this barnyard fowl to become a staple in many a country's cooking will never be known. Only one thing is for sure—the chicken is here to stay. As the dejected rooster said in a Mark Fenderson cartoon: "What's the use? Yesterday an egg, tomorrow a feather duster."

When I was a child, security to me was a cache of licorice. At eighteen I felt delightfully wicked sipping my first absinthe; I discovered the Greek licorice-flavored aperitif *ouzo* long before it became fashionable and will in late October serve licorice ice cream for dessert. With a past like that, it was inevitable for me to try and add my favorite flavor to food. This chicken recipe is one of the results:

CHICKEN ANISE
(4-6 Servings)

4	chicken breasts
4	drum sticks
12	large mushrooms, washed and quartered
8	small white onions, peeled
½	cup butter or margarine
1	1 lb. 12 oz. can tomatoes
1	6 oz. can tomato paste
⅓	cup flour
1¾	cup chicken broth
¾	cup dry white wine or sherry
1	tsp. sweet basil
½	tsp. anise seed
1-2	tsp. salt
1	6 oz. pkg. saffron rice
1	10 oz. pkg. frozen peas

Sauté the washed and quartered mushrooms with the peeled onions in half the butter for about 5-10 minutes and set aside. Dust the chicken pieces with flour and brown until golden in remaining butter. Add the mushrooms and onions to the chicken pieces, together with tomatoes, tomato paste, broth, wine, basil, anise and salt. Stir lightly, bring to a boil and let simmer, after you've reduced heat, for 45 minutes under cover. Add the saffron rice and continue simmering, covered for another 15 minutes. Add the peas, give the pot a good stir, and in another 15 minutes' time of covered simmering, the dish is ready to serve.

Serve with a crisp green salad, hard-crust rolls and a bottle of chilled vin rosé.

If some is left over and you reheat it the next day, check carefully for bones. With lengthy cooking they have a tendency to leave the meat.

The following is a slight variation of the standard Coq au Vin . . . a little pale in looks, so a lettuce and tomato salad spruces it up nicely, as does a bottle of vin rosé.

NOTES

BRANDIED CHICKEN
(6 Servings)

2	2-3 lb. broilers, cut in pieces
¼	cup flour
1	tsp. salt
¼	tsp. white pepper
2	tbs. butter
2	tbs. olive oil
6	whole green onions, chopped
3	carrots, 1″ pieces
12	small white onions, peeled
½	cup brandy
1¼	cup dry white wine
1	tbs. parsley flakes
12	large mushroom caps

Coat the chicken pieces with the flour to which you have added the salt and pepper.

Heat 1 tbs. *each* of the butter and olive oil in the pot and brown the chicken pieces, quickly, on both sides. Remove from pan, add the remaining butter and olive oil and sauté green onions, carrots and white onions for 5-10 minutes over low heat. Return the chicken pieces to the pot and stir. Flame the brandy and pour into pot together with white wine and parsley. Cover and simmer until chicken is done, approximately 30-40 minutes. During the last 15 minutes add the mushroom caps.

It was after due deliberation I named the following Chinese-inspired dish a stew rather than give it a fancy Chinese name, mainly to assure you that it does serve as a full meal. Should you be haunted by that old superstition that Chinese food leaves you hungry in an hour, take the advice as put forth in verse by Eugene Field:

> *No matter what conditions*
> *Dyspeptic come to feaze,*
> *The best of all physicians*
> *Is apple pie and cheese . . .*

and follow the stew by just that.

NOTES

CHINESE CHICKEN STEW
(4-6 Servings)

3	lbs. chicken, cut in pieces
1	tbs. olive oil
½	tsp. salt
2	tsp. powdered ginger
¼	cup brandy
¾	cup boiling water
1	1 lb. 4 oz. can bamboo shoots, 2″ pieces, drained
½	lb. fresh mushrooms, cleaned and sliced
1	8 oz. can water chestnuts, drained and sliced
4	green onions, cut in 2″ pieces, tops and all
2	tbs. soy sauce
2	tbs. cornstarch
1	tbs. sugar
¼	cup water
	Chinese noodles

In a pot, sauté the chicken pieces in hot oil over medium heat until well browned. Add the salt, ginger and brandy and cook, covered, over low heat for 10 minutes. Add the boiling water and continue simmering, under cover, for another 30 minutes. Remove chicken and keep warm.

Now add the drained and cut bamboo shoots, mushrooms, water chestnuts and green onions. Bring to a boil, reduce heat and let simmer for 10 minutes before adding the cornstarch, sugar and soy sauce all blended with the ¼ cup water. Increase heat a little and continue cooking for 5 minutes, stirring constantly, until sauce is thickened. Add the chicken pieces, and let just heat through before you serve with Chinese noodles.

What follows is the standard Coq au Vin. Try and serve it with Cheese Bread . . . slices of French bread, buttered and covered by a mild cheese such as Swiss or Jack, heated for 5 minutes in a 400° oven. A raw spinach salad and a bottle of vin rosé complete the picture.

NOTES

COQ AU VIN
(4 Servings)

¼	lb. salt pork
4	green onions, sliced
8	small white onions, peeled
1	clove garlic, minced
2	carrots, in chunks
5-6	lbs. chicken, cut in serving pieces
¼	cup flour
1-2	tsp. salt
½	tsp. pepper
½	tsp. dried thyme
1	cup dry red wine
½	tsp. crumbled bay leaves
½	lb. fresh mushrooms, washed and sliced
1	tbs. parsley flakes

Dice the salt pork and brown lightly in pot. Discard the pork and add to the drippings the green and white onions, together with the carrots and garlic. Sauté for about 5 minutes and set vegetables aside on a plate.

In a paper bag, dust the chicken pieces with the flour, salt, pepper and thyme. Brown chicken in the fat remaining in pot before adding the precooked vegetables, wine and bay leaves. Simmer, covered, for about 35 minutes. Add the washed and sliced mushrooms and continue simmering for another 5-10 minutes.

If you don't think this sounds much different from the Brandied Chicken, try it anyway, paying tribute to Roland Young's words:

> *And here's the happy bounding flea . . .*
> *You cannot tell the he from she.*
> *The sexes look alike you see;*
> *But she can tell, and so can he.*

The following recipe is a little on the sweet side, so save it for your more sweetly inclined friends.

NOTES

FRUITY CHICKEN
(3-4 Servings)

2	lbs. chicken breasts and thighs
4	tbs. lime juice
¼	cup flour
1	tsp. salt
¼	tsp. black pepper
3	tbs. butter
3	tbs. olive oil
1	large onion, chopped
1	cup crushed pineapple, drained
3	med. tomatoes, diced
3	tbs. currants
2	tbs. brown sugar
4	tbs. rum
	Chinese noodles

Dip the chicken pieces in lime juice and lightly coat with flour seasoned with salt and pepper. In a pot, heat the butter and olive oil and brown chicken pieces well on all sides. Add the finely chopped onion and cook for 5 minutes, stirring occasionally. Add the drained pineapple, diced tomatoes, currants and brown sugar. Blend well and let simmer over low heat, covered, for about 30 minutes or until, with a fork, the chicken feels done. Stir in the rum and serve over Chinese noodles.

If you serve the following dish to your fellow, and he says he doesn't like it, all you'll know is that he isn't much to cook for.

HEARTY CHICKEN STEW
(4 Servings)

3	lbs. chicken cut in serving pieces
3	tsp. salt
1	tsp. MSG
¼	cup butter or margarine
2	med. onions, sliced
1	20 oz. can tomatoes
1	6 oz. can tomato paste
1	cup dry white wine
1	cup water
2-3	chicken bouillon cubes
1	inner heart celery, sliced, leaves and all, about 1-1½ cups.
½	tsp. thyme
½	tsp. marjoram
½	tsp. sweet basil
1	12 oz. can whole kernel corn, drained
1	10 oz. pkg. frozen lima beans

Sprinkle the chicken pieces with salt and MSG. In a large pot, melt the butter and brown the chicken well on all sides. Remove chicken and add the onions, browning them lightly. Return the chicken pieces to the pot together with tomatoes, tomato paste, wine, water, bouillon cubes and the remaining 2 tsp. salt (*or to taste*—the bouillon cubes are a little salty) and the herbs. Mix lightly, bring to a boil, reduce heat and simmer, covered, for about 40 minutes. Mix in the drained corn and lima beans and continue simmering, under cover for another 20 minutes.

Have plenty of crusty bread on hand to sop up the juices, bring out that trusty chilled vin rosé, and enjoy.

The following is truly a dish fixed in a jiffy. From the very start it takes only 30 minutes. If you want to complete the Japanese mood, serve it with sake, seating your guests on pillows on the floor around your coffee table.

NOTES

JAPANESE CHICKEN
(4-6 Servings)

4	lbs. chicken, boned and skinned in advance
6	dried Chinese mushrooms
1	cup warm water
4	cups chicken broth
1	tbs. soy sauce
1	tbs. MSG
1	med. head Chinese cabbage, sliced
1	10½ oz. can bamboo shoots, thinly sliced
	Chinese noodles

SAUCE

5	white radishes, grated
¼	cup soy sauce
2	tsp. lemon juice
	dash of cayenne

Cut the boned and skinned chicken into slivers while the mushrooms are soaking in the warm water. After 20 minutes, drain the mushrooms and snip into quarters with your kitchen scissors.

In a deep skillet or pot, combine the chicken broth, soy sauce and MSG. Bring to a boil and add the slivered chicken. Reduce heat and simmer for about 15 minutes. Add the cabbage, bamboo shoots and mushrooms and simmer for an additional 5 minutes before you serve, in deep, pretty Japanese bowls.

If your guests are accomplished chopstick eaters, they'll lift their own servings out of the pot, dipping the mouthfuls into individual servings of the sauce you made by mixing the finely grated radishes with soy sauce and lemon juice. If they haven't mastered the chopsticks, simply ladle the chicken into the plates, pass the sauce around and

have some Chinese noodles on hand for those who might
care for that. Serve warm sake from dainty little cups,
either way and encourage your guests to try the chopsticks. As Jonathan Swift said: "Fingers were made before
forks, and hands before knives."

The next two recipes both hail from South of the
Border. Whether or not they were inspired by the sup-
posed mañana, mañana attitude prevailing there, I cannot say, but both should be prepared in advance.

The Baked Chicken should be allowed to sit and steep
in its heated juices for at least 2 hours before finishing it,
and the Chicken Divan must spend 24 hours in the refrigerator, gathering flavor, before heating. But both are
worth planning ahead for.

MEXICAN BAKED CHICKEN
(4-6 Servings)

4	whole chicken breasts, split
4-6	drumsticks
	Flour
½	cup olive oil
3	large tomatoes, quartered
1	cup blanched slivered almonds
1	med. green pepper, diced
¾	cup seedless raisins
1	14 oz. can chunk pineapple, drained
½	cup dry white wine
1	can undiluted beef broth
1	tsp. salt
¼	tsp. nutmeg
¼	tsp. allspice
¼	tsp. black pepper
	Flour tortillas

Dust the chicken pieces with flour. In a large pot or deep baking dish, heat the oil and brown the chicken well on all sides. Remove chicken and add the quartered tomatoes, sautéing them for 5 minutes before you add the almonds, green pepper, raisins, pineapple, white wine, beef broth, salt, pepper and spices. Bring to a boil, reduce heat and let simmer for 5 minutes, then turn the heat off. Completely submerge the chicken pieces in the sauce, cover the dish and let it stand for at least 2 hours; bake, covered, in a 375° oven for 1 hour or until chicken is tender. Serve with flour tortillas that have been heated in the oven for the last 10 minutes. Butter them at the table!

This is the recipe you fix 24 hours before you plan to serve it. Make sure your kitchen work space is neat and unencumbered. The assembly of this dish requires at least one medium-size bowl and enough room for three little heaps of tortillas, vegetables and cheese spread out on wax paper.

NOTES

MEXICAN CHICKEN DIVAN
(4-6 Servings)

4	whole chicken breasts
1	doz. corn tortillas
2	cans cream of chicken soup
1	cup milk
2	small cans green chile salsa
¼	tsp. allspice
¼	tsp. nutmeg
¼	tsp. cinnamon
2	green peppers, diced
12	mushrooms, quartered
1	lb. Cheddar cheese, grated
2	tbs. water
	Butter or margarine

Wrap the individual chicken breasts in foil and bake them for about 1 hour in a 400° oven. (Since this should be done the day before you serve this dish, try and take advantage of something else you might already have going in the oven.) Mix the soup with the milk, salsa and spices. Clean and dice the green pepper, wash and quarter the mushrooms. Cut the tortillas into ½″ strips . . . keeping the vegetables and tortillas separate. Grate the cheese and make a separate mound out of that as well. Generously butter a large baking dish and wet the bottom with the water. When the chicken is tender and cool enough to handle, remove all skin and bones and tear into bite-size pieces.

In the bottom of your large baking dish, arrange a layer of tortilla strips and cover the strips with half the chicken meat, on top of which you put half the green pepper and mushroom supply. Over this pour half the soup-and-salsa mixture and start all over again with a layer of tortillas, followed by chicken, pepper and mushrooms, and soup. Sprinkle generously with the grated cheese, cover tightly, and allow to sit in refrigerator for 24 hours.

Three hours before you plan to serve it, remove the dish from the refrigerator. In another 1 hour and 30 minutes, put it in a 300° oven and allow to bake for 1 hour to 1 hour and 30 minutes, uncovered. Serve this with chilled beer and a tomato and avocado salad.

The next is a good dish for a raw winter evening, and it should be accompanied by a crisp green salad. In making your salad dressing, remember the Spanish proverb that: "Four persons are wanted to make a good salad: a spend-thrift for oil, a miser for vinegar, a counselor for salt, and a madman to stir it all up."

CHICKEN RICE POT
(4-6 Servings)

2½	lbs. your favorite chicken pieces
¼	cup flour
1	tsp. salt
¼	tsp. black pepper
8	slices bacon
1½	cups raw rice
1	1¾ oz. dry cream of leek soup mix
4	carrots, cut in chunks
2	med. onions, sliced
1	tsp. tarragon
3	tbs. parsley flakes
1	cup dry white wine
3	cups water
3	chicken bouillon cubes

Dust the chicken pieces with salt and pepper-seasoned flour. Fry the bacon to a crisp in a large kettle or Dutch oven. Remove bacon and drain on paper towels. Brown the chicken pieces, a few at a time, in the bacon drippings and remove to a plate. Add the rice and soup mix to the pot and brown. Stir in the carrots and onions together with the tarragon and parsley.

Place the chicken pieces on top of this mixture and crumble the bacon over all. Add the water, wine and bouillon cubes, cover and simmer for about 1 hour after you've brought mixture to a boil and reduce heat. The dish is done when the chicken is tender and the rice has absorbed the liquid.

The following recipe deserves not only your prettiest covered baking dish, but also favorite people as guests— "friends," who in the words of Richard Kirk, "are thrice blessed: they come, they stay, and presently they go away."

CHICKEN ROSEMARY
(6 Servings)

4	med. potatoes, pared and halved
4	carrots, in chunks
2	med. white turnips, pared and quartered
1	green pepper, in strips
2	stalks celery with leaves, 1″ pieces
6	white small onions, peeled
12	large mushrooms, washed and halved
3	tomatoes, thickly sliced
4	slices of bacon
4	lbs. chicken, cut in serving pieces
½	tsp. crumbled bay leaves
1	tsp. rosemary, crushed
½	cup dry white wine

After you've prepared all of the vegetables, get out a large pretty pot or casserole, about 3 qt. capacity; line its bottom with the bacon, place the chicken pieces on top, sprinkle with salt and pepper and arrange the mixed vegetables on top of that, reserving the tomato slices for the very top. Sprinkle with rosemary and bay leaves, pour the wine over all, and bake, covered, at 375° for 1 hour and 30 minutes.

Serve with crusty bread and a chilled vin rosé, and everybody will agree with Shakespeare's line: "There's rosemary . . . that's for remembrance."

If you serve the next dish at the darkest of wintertime when you doubt that spring will ever come again, I guarantee you that the flavors of this stew will restore your faith in the arrival of budding trees and daffodils and crocuses.

SPRING CHICKEN STEW
(4 Servings)

2-3	lbs. chicken breasts and thighs
1	tsp. salt
¼	tsp. pepper
¼	cup butter or margarine
1	med. onion, chopped
¼	cup water
¼	cup dry sherry
1	chicken bouillon cube
½	tsp. dried mint leaves
1	1 lb. can whole kernel corn; drain but reserve liquid
1	10 oz. pkg. frozen peas
½	tsp. grated lemon peel
2	tbs. lemon juice
1	cup sour cream

Sprinkle the chicken with salt and pepper and brown well on all sides in heated butter. Add the finely chopped onion, together with water, sherry, chicken bouillon cube and dried mint and simmer, covered, for about 30 minutes or until chicken is tender. Remove chicken pieces from pot and keep warm . . . wrapping them in foil and placing them in the unlit oven should do the trick. Add the corn with about 2 tbs. of the liquid, the frozen peas, lemon peel and juice and heat for about 10 minutes. Return the chicken pieces to the pot together with the sour cream, heating everything to just before boiling.

Serve with marinated tomato slices and a chilled white wine.

Before you start fixing this Paella—which I like to believe is just different enough from the more standard versions to make it very special—make sure you have a real large pot on hand. Not only does it call for a lot of ingredients—some of them rather bulky—but the rice expands as you know.

There's quite a lot of work involved in preparing this, but it's worth every second. In the words of Franz Kafka: "There are two cardinal sins from which all others spring: impatience and laziness."

If you have either of those traits, don't start this dish.

PAELLA
(6-8 Servings)

1	cup olive oil
2	med. onions, chopped
3½	lbs. of chicken, cut into serving pieces
4	lbs. duck, cut into serving pieces
½	lb. pork, cubed
3	chorizos, sliced
4	tomatoes, wedged
1	green pepper, sliced
2	cans consomme undiluted
1	cup dry white wine
1½	cups bottled clam juice
1	beef bouillon cube
2	tsp. salt
½	tsp. marjoram
1	tsp. saffron
1½	cups raw rice
1	10 oz. pkg. frozen green beans
1	10 oz. pkg. frozen green peas
1	small head cauliflower, picked into flowerettes
12	jumbo shrimp, shelled and deveined
1	pkg. frozen lobster tails, cut into bite-size pieces

In a very large kettle or Dutch oven, heat the olive oil and sauté the chopped onion until translucent, about 5 minutes. Remove from pot and set aside. Now brown the chicken, duck and cubed pork well on all sides. You'll probably have to do a few at a time, making sure that, with the duck, you've cut off any excess fat and skin.

When all the meat is done, return the onions to the pot together with the sliced chorizos, tomato wedges, the sliced green pepper, consomme, white wine, clam juice and bouillon cube. Sprinkle the salt and spices over all, stir lightly, bring to a boil, reduce heat and let simmer for 20 minutes or so. Now add the raw rice, cauliflower and defrosted frozen vegetables, mix lightly, cover and bake in a 350° oven for 1 hour. Stir in the shrimp and lobster pieces and continue baking, covered, for another 15 minutes. If the mixture turns a little dry, add a little water as necessary.

If you start this ahead of time or the day before, stop before you add the rice and the ingredients that follow with that. The next day you bring the pot to a slight boil before adding the rice.

This is a great dish for a buffet. Have on hand plenty of hard-crust rolls and chilled vin rosé, but also a good mixed green salad, paying homage to Robert Louis Stevenson's words:

> *Let first the onion flourish there,*
> *Rose among roots, the maiden-fair*
> *Wine-scented and poetic soul*
> *Of the capacious salad bowl.*

Duck seems to be a far more popular fowl in Europe than here, but even though you might have your fears about its greasiness, try it in this stew. You might change your mind about this wonderful bird.

FRENCH DUCK STEW
(4 Servings)

5	lbs. duck, cut into serving pieces
1	med. onion, chopped
¼	lb. smoked ham, cubed
3	cups consomme
2-3	tsp. salt
½	tsp. pepper
¼	cup sherry
1	tbs. parsley flakes
1	lb. fresh rutabagas, pared and quartered
8	small white onions, peeled
1	tsp. thyme
½	tsp. sweet basil
1	10 oz. pkg. frozen peas

After you've trimmed off excess fat and skin from the pieces of duck, put a large kettle or Dutch oven on the stove and in that, over medium heat, brown the pieces of duck well on all sides. This takes about 30 minutes since you want to melt off as much fat as possible. Drain the melted duck grease from the pot, add the chopped onion and let it sauté for about 5 minutes in the grease that sticks to the pot, pushing the pieces of duck aside while you do this.

Add the cubed ham, sprinkle with salt, pepper and parsley and pour the consomme and sherry over all. Give a good stir, bring to a boil, reduce heat and let simmer for about 30 minutes. Skim off any fat that may have risen to the surface before you add the rutabagas, onions, thyme and basil. Stir and simmer for an additional 30 minutes, then add the peas and you're ready to serve in about 15 minutes. If you prefer, you can bake the dish in a 375° oven for the overall length of time.

Serve with a dry red wine, a tangy salad and hard-crust rolls.

LAMB

The lamb seems to be taking a back seat to its fellow domestic quadrupeds both as far as literature and cooking are concerned.

Aside from "Mary Had a Little Lamb," which I guess most of us remember having to recite to doting grandparents, and Kipling's "We're Poor Little Lambs Who've Lost Our Way . . . ," which to my generation at least was an integral part of college beer parties, I have not been able to find one example of the lamb having moved anybody to poetic praise.

Culinarily speaking, the same is more or less the sad truth. Most people have only an occasional lamb chop or leg of lamb, and that's a situation I'd like to rectify with the following recipes, inspired in part by the Near and Far East where the lamb is truly appreciated for its subtle flavor.

This first recipe includes the basic ingredients of Greek cooking, namely lamb, mint and lemon juice, spruced up by adding artichoke hearts and wine. If you put either "Never on Sunday" or "Zorba the Greek" on the stereo, accompany the dish with crusty bread and feta cheese—a goat cheese available in groceries specializing in foreign products—and chilled Retsina, a Greek wine seasoned with pine needles, you may experience a teleportation to a tavern in Athens.

LAMB AND ARTICHOKES A LA GREQUE
(4-6 Servings)

2-3	lbs. boned leg of lamb, cubed
2	med. onions, sliced
½	tsp. dried mint
½	tsp. anise seed
1	tsp. salt
¼	tsp. white pepper
½	cup dry white wine
½	cup water
3-4	tbs. olive oil
1	beef bouillon cube
2	10 oz. pkgs. frozen artichoke hearts, thawed out
2	tbs. lemon juice

Heat the oil in the pot and sauté the sliced onions for about 5 minutes or until translucent. Push aside, add the cubed lamb and brown well on all sides. Mix together, sprinkle with herbs, salt and pepper, add the bouillon cube and pour the wine and water over all. Bring to a boil, reduce heat and let simmer, covered, for 1 hour. Add the thawed-out artichoke hearts together with the lemon juice and continue simmering for another 20 minutes at which time you can carry a truly delightful dish to either the dinner table or your buffet.

Serve with crusty rolls and feta cheese.

The same friend who gave me the recipe for the Kima also supplied me with his version of Lamb Curry, Java-style. He served it with exotic condiments brought with him from Java, but the standard U.S. substitutes will do very nicely.

LAMB CURRY
(4 Servings)

2	lbs. boneless lamb, in 1″ cubes
2	tbs. butter or margarine
1	Bermuda onion, chopped
1	large stalk celery, with leaves, chopped
1	green pepper, chopped
2	cups chicken broth
¾	cup raw rice
2	tbs. curry *or to taste*
¼	tsp. ground ginger
¼	tsp. turmeric
½	cup seedless raisins
1	tsp. salt
¼	tsp. white pepper
¼	cup yogurt
2	tbs. heavy cream

In the pot heat the butter and brown the lamb cubes, making sure they're well done on all sides. Add the chopped onion and let that get lightly brown. Now stir in the chopped green pepper, celery, chicken broth and rice. Bring to a boil, reduce heat, and let simmer, covered, for 15 minutes. Now stir in the curry, together with ginger, turmeric, raisins, salt and pepper. Cover and simmer for another 15 minutes or until meat is tender. Remove the pot from the heat and stir in the yogurt and cream mixed together.

Serve with condiments such as chopped scallions, tomato wedges, chopped hard-boiled eggs, chutney and flaked coconut. Some crumbled bacon and salty, chopped peanuts are nice too.

The Greeks do something marvelous with lamb, eggplant, and cheese sauces, called Moussaka. However, no matter how hard I tried, it wasn't possible to adapt it into a one-pot recipe. But to get the benefit of the eggplant-and-lamb combination, try this version of curried lamb.

CURRIED LAMB AND EGGPLANT
(6-8 Servings)

4	lbs. lamb stew meat
2	tsp. salt
½	tsp. black pepper
¼	cup flour
3-4	tbs. olive oil
1	large eggplant, pared and diced
2	large onions, sliced
2	tart apples, diced
4	celery stalks, diced
3	tsp. curry *or to taste*
½	cup dry white wine
½	cup water
2	beef bouillon cubes
2	large tomatoes, in wedges
½	cup pine nuts

In a paper bag mix the flour with salt and pepper and shake the cubed meat in this until nicely coated. Heat the oil in a large pot and brown the flour-covered meat well on all sides. Add the diced eggplant, sliced onions, diced apples and celery; stir lightly, sprinkle with curry, tuck in the bouillon cubes and pour the wine and water over all. Bring to a slow boil, reduce heat and let simmer for 1 hour. Now add the tomato wedges and pine nuts and let simmer for another 15 minutes or so until meat is fork tender. A bottle of chilled white wine goes well with this.

Somebody once said: "If you can make your guests feel at home when you wish they were, you're a good hostess." If you serve them either of the following two French-inspired dishes, I give you fair warning that they might want to stay for any possible leftovers the next day. Here again these recipes do double duty. You can serve them either as dinner or part of a buffet.

FRENCH LAMB STEW
(4-6 Servings)

2	lbs. lamb stew meat, cubed
2	tbs. olive oil
2	tsp. sugar
1	tsp. salt
¼	tsp. white pepper
3	tbs. flour
2	large tomatoes, in wedges
½	tsp. thyme
½	tsp. crumbled bay leaves
1½	cup dry white wine
½	cup water
2	beef bouillon cubes
6	med. potatoes, pared and cut in halves
6	carrots, scraped, in chunks
2	small turnips, pared and quartered
8	small white onions, peeled
1	10 oz. pkg. frozen green beans, thawed out
1	10 oz. pkg. frozen lima beans, thawed out

In a large pot, heat the oil and brown the meat well on all sides before you sprinkle it with sugar, salt and pepper; continue cooking the meat for another 5 minutes and then sprinkle it with the flour. Add the tomatoes, thyme and bay leaves, the bouillon cubes, part of the wine and water. The liquid should just cover the meat. Bring to a boil, cover and bake in a 375° oven for 1 hour and 30 minutes.

Add the prepared potatoes, carrots, turnips and onions and continue baking for another 30 minutes or until the vegetables are almost tender. Add the lima and green beans which have thawed out during all of the above. Stir mixture well, cover and continue baking for another 15 minutes.

Serve with hard rolls and a chilled vin rosé.

As you may have noticed, I use garlic rather sparingly, which is simply a personal preference that shouldn't deter you from trying it where you think it will work. I once read a statement by Lynn White, Jr., a president of Mills College, in which he said: "Free speech is like garlic. If you are perfectly sure of yourself, you enjoy it and your friends tolerate it." I have a tendency to agree with that thought; however, in the following recipe I wouldn't be without it.

NOTES

LAMB AND KIDNEY RAGOUT
(4-6 Servings)

2½	lbs. shoulder of lamb, 1″ cubes
6	lamb kidneys, cleaned and halved
¼	cup flour
3	tbs. butter or margarine
2	tsp. salt
½	tsp. black pepper
½	tsp. thyme
½	tsp. dried mint
¾	tsp. rosemary
1	13 oz. can chicken broth
1	6 oz. can tomato paste
½	cup vin rose
4	med.-size turnips, pared and quartered
8	small white onions, peeled
3	med. carrots, 1″ pieces
1	clove garlic, crushed
1	green pepper, seeded and cut in strips
2	leeks, 1″ pieces
1	10 oz. pkg. frozen artichoke hearts, thawed out
2	med. tomatoes, in wedges

Coat the cubed lamb and cleaned kidney pieces in flour by shaking them in a bag. In a large pot, melt butter, add the flour-coated lamb, *not* the kidneys, and brown well on all sides. Sprinkle with salt and pepper and dried herbs, and pour the tomato paste, chicken broth and vin rosé over all. Bring to a boil, reduce heat and simmer, covered for 45 minutes, while you clean and prepare the vegetables.

Now add the reserved flour-coated kidney pieces, together with turnips, onions, carrots, green pepper, leeks and crushed garlic. Give it all a good stir and continue simmering, under cover, for another 30 minutes. Now add the thawed-out artichoke hearts together with the tomato wedges and simmer for another 15 minutes. If you feel the dish is too juicy you can leave the cover off during this last stage.

Serve with warm rolls and a chilled vin rosé.

From Morocco, across the Mediterranean, comes the next recipe. The flavors are subtle, but don't leave out any of the ingredients, not even if you feel saffron is a little expensive.

Like Kipling's definition of the feminine "it": " 'Tisn't beauty so to speak, nor good talk necessarily. It's just IT. Some women'll stay in a man's memory if they once walked down a street . . ." this dish will linger happily in your memory.

MOROCCAN LAMB STEW
(4-6 Servings)

2	med. onions, cut in eighths
2	tbs. olive oil
2½	lbs. lamb, cubed
¼	cup olive oil
1	med. onion, chopped
2-3	tsp. salt
¾	tsp. black pepper
½	tsp. crumbled bay leaves
1	whole clove
3	tbs. parsley flakes
½	tsp. powdered saffron
½	tsp. ground ginger
2	large tomatoes, chopped
½	cup dry white wine
1	cup seedless raisins, plumped in warm water
⅓	cup slivered almonds
4	hard-boiled eggs, cut in halves

Heat the 2 tbs. of olive oil in a pot and sauté the 2 onions cut in eighths in this until golden, about 5 minutes. Remove onion sections and set aside. Add the ¼ cup oil to pot, heat, and brown the cubed lamb well on all sides. Stir in the chopped onion together with all the spices and the chopped tomatoes. Let simmer for a couple of minutes before adding the white wine. Now cover and let dish simmer for about 1 hour or until lamb is tender. Now add the precooked onion sections together with the raisins which have soaked in warm water for 30 minutes; sprinkle the slivered almonds on top and bake, uncovered, in a 450° oven for 15 minutes or until most of the liquid has evaporated.

Place the hard-boiled egg halves on top and serve with crusty bread, feta cheese and a chilled white wine.

The following is a slightly sweeter version from the Arab world.

ARABIAN LAMB STEW
(4 Servings)

1½	lbs. lamb, cubed
2	med. onions, chopped
4	tbs. olive oil
1	6 oz. can tomato paste
¼	cup dry white wine
2	tbs. brandy
2	large tomatoes, quartered
1-2	tsp. salt
¼	tsp. white pepper
¼	cup dried apricot halves
¼	cup dried peach halves
¼	cup seedless raisins
¼	cup dried prunes, chopped
¼	tsp. ground coriander
⅛	tsp. turmeric
3	tbs. pine nuts
2	tsp. salted almonds

Have the meat cubed in bite-size pieces. Heat the oil in the pot and sauté the onion for about 5 minutes or until translucent. Remove onion from pot, add meat and brown well on all sides. Mix in the sautéed onion together with the tomato paste, wine, brandy, quartered tomatoes, dried fruits and spices. Simmer, covered for 1 hour. Add pine nuts, stirring slightly, and continue cooking for another 5 minutes.

Serve with almonds sprinkled on top and a dry white wine; follow with a well-assorted cheese tray.

If you would like to go a little plainer try the next two recipes—one is for lamb stew; the other is a savory way of cooking a whole leg of lamb in one pot. I never attempt the latter without somebody on hand who can carve.

OLD-FASHIONED LAMB STEW
(4 Servings)

1	large onion, sliced
2	tbs. olive oil
1½	lbs. lamb stew, cubed
4	tbs. flour
1	tsp. salt
¼	tsp. pepper
1	cup dry sherry
1½	cups water
2	beef bouillon cubes
1	tsp. dried dill weed
2-3	large potatoes, pared and thickly sliced
2-3	large carrots, in chunks
1	10 oz. pkg. frozen peas
	Parsley

Sauté the sliced onion in the heated oil until translucent, but not brown. Add the cubed meat, sprinkle with
flour, salt and pepper, and cook for 5 minutes, stirring all
the time. The meat should simply turn gray, not brown.
Add water, sherry, bouillon cubes and dill, cooking and
stirring until slightly thickened, but not lumpy. Cover and
simmer for 1 hour. Add the potatoes and carrots, cover
and simmer for another 20 minutes; then add the peas and
cook for 15 minutes more.

Sprinkle parsley on top and serve with sourdough bread
and foamy beer.

POTTED LEG OF LAMB
(4-6 Servings)

4	lbs. leg of lamb, whole
2-3	tbs. olive oil
2	med. onions, diced
1	heart of celery, diced
3	med. carrots, sliced
4	med. potatoes, pared and quartered
2	tsp. parsley
¾	tsp. dried dill
½	tsp. oregano
½	cup dry red wine
1½	cups water
2	beef bouillon cubes
2	tsp. salt
½	tsp. black pepper

In a large kettle or Dutch oven, heat the oil and brown the whole leg of lamb well on all sides. Pack the prepared vegetables down around it, sprinkle with herbs, salt and pepper, tuck the bouillon cubes and pour wine and water over all. Cover tightly and simmer for about 2 hours or until meat is tender.

Lift the leg of lamb from the pot and carve on board, serving the vegetables right from the pot.

If you like thicker gravy, you may blend ¼ cup of flour with 1 tbs. of water and add it to the pot after you've removed the lamb. Cook, stirring, until the sauce is thickened.

Serve with individual little loaves of bread now available in the freezer section of your market, a tangy cucumber salad and wine, either rosé or white.

In case you liked the Curried Lamb and Eggplant, try this Turkish dish which combines not only the same two main ingredients, but also some tantalizing spices.

NOTES

TURKISH LAMB
(4-6 Servings)

4	lbs. boneless lamb, in 1″ cubes
	Flour
2	tbs. butter or margarine
2	tbs. olive oil
½	tsp. crumbled bay leaves
⅛	tsp. ground cloves
⅛	tsp. cinnamon
1½	cups beef broth
3	tbs. lemon juice
2	tsp. salt
½	tsp. white pepper
1	large onion, chopped
¼	tsp. thyme
1	med. eggplant pared and cubed
¼	tsp. dried mint
1	green pepper, seeded and cut in strips
¼	tsp. oregano
2	large tomatoes, in wedges

In a pot, melt the butter and heat with olive oil. In this, brown well on all sides the lightly floured cubed lamb; when done, sprinkle with bay leaves, cloves, cinnamon, salt and pepper before pouring the consomme and lemon juice over all. Bring to a slow boil, reduce heat and simmer, covered, for 45 minutes. Add your chopped vegetables in layers, sprinkling each with the herb called for, and topping it all off with the wedges of tomato. Cover pot and bake in a 350° oven for 1 hour.

Before serving, give the pot a good stir and set proudly on the table. A dry red wine goes well with this.

If you want to start this ahead of time, stop before you come to the vegetable part, doing that 1 hour before you plan to serve.

If you're ever faced with some leftover meat from a leg of lamb, do me a favor and try the following recipe. It's one of the tastiest ways of serving leftovers and goes over very well with men.

NOTES

TASTY LEFTOVER LAMB
(4 Servings)

1	med. green pepper, seeded and diced
1	small onion, diced
¼	cup butter or margarine
¼	cup flour
1	tsp. salt
¼	tsp. white pepper
½	tsp. dill weed
1⅓	cups milk
⅔	cup dry sherry
2	cups diced, cooked lamb
2	med. potatoes, cooked and cubed
8	fresh mushrooms, sliced
1	pimento, diced
½	cup grated American cheese

In an ovenproof baking dish (Is there any other kind?) sauté the green pepper and onion until translucent, about 5 minutes. Stir in flour, add milk and sherry and cook, stirring constantly, until thickened. Season with salt, pepper and dill. Add all the other ingredients, except the cheese. Mix well and sprinkle with the grated cheese. Bake in a 375° oven for about 15 minutes until the dish is heated through and the cheese bubbly golden.

Here I, of course, assumed that you had some potatoes left over from the leg of lamb dinner. If that's not the case, dice two potatoes and sauté them with the green pepper and onion and proceed as above.

A crisp green salad and cheese breadsticks go very nicely with this.

PORK

Ogden Nash once wrote:

> *The pig, if I am not mistaken,*
> *supplies us sausage, ham, and bacon.*
> *Let others say his heart is big . . .*
> *I call it stupid of the pig.*

Lovers of the hearty breakfast will probably take strong issue with Mr. Nash and his point of view—there is hardly anything more invigorating than the aroma of bacon wafting through the house in the morning—but Mr. Nash also neglected to mention that the pig does furnish us with other palatable cuts, a fact that's no more appreciated anywhere in the world than in Denmark.

Taking to heart Shakespeare's line from *The Merchant of Venice:* "This making of Christians will raise the price of hogs . . ." the Danes not only derive a major part of their national income from exporting pork products, they've also made pork the mainstay of their diet.

On the following pages you can see for yourself the imagination they bring to the preparation of pork chops.

DANISH SWEET AND SOUR PORK CHOPS
(4 Servings)

6	lean pork chops
2	tbs. butter or margarine
1	tsp. curry powder
2	cups water (to cover)
2	chicken bouillon cubes
6	med. potatoes, pared and halved
1	tsp. salt
¼	tsp. black pepper
10	pitted prunes
4	tart apples, cored and quartered
1	tsp. sugar, *or to taste*
2	tsp. vinegar

In a pot or deep skillet, brown the chops in the bubbling butter into which you have blended the curry. When the chops are nicely browned on both sides, add the halved potatoes, sprinkle with salt and pepper, drop in the bouillon cubes and pour the water over all. The water should just cover the mixture. Simmer, covered, for 45 minutes after it is brought to a boil. During the last 10-15 minutes add the prunes and apples, and continue simmering without cover to get rid of excess liquid. Just before serving, mix in sugar and vinegar.

Serve with crusty bread, marinated tomato slices and a mug of beer.

HEARTY PORK CHOPS AND CABBAGE
(4-6 Servings)

6	lean pork chops
1	med. onion, chopped
2	tbs. butter or margarine
1	cup V-8 vegetable juice
¼	cup cider vinegar
2	tbs. soy sauce
1	tbs. sugar
1	tsp. salt
¼	tsp. white pepper
½	tsp. sweet basil
¼	tsp. caraway seed
1	med. head white cabbage, shredded

In a pot or large skillet, brown the chops well on both sides in the melted butter. Add the chopped onion, vegetable juice, vinegar, soy sauce, sugar, salt, pepper, basil and caraway seed. Stir well; bring to a slow boil, reduce heat and simmer for 30 minutes under cover. Add the shredded cabbage, tossing well to make sure cabbage is coated with the sauce, and simmer for another 15 minutes, covered.

Serve with slices of rye bread and foamy beer.

This is the kind of recipe that brings to mind the old saying:

> *Give me a good digestion, Lord,*
> *And also something to digest.*

PORK CHOPS JARDINIERE
(4-6 Servings)

6	lean pork chops
4	med. potatoes, pared and quartered
4-6	carrots, in chunks
1	cup water
1	chicken bouillon cube
½	cup dry vermouth
¼	tsp. fenugreek or curry powder
¼	tsp. white pepper
½	tsp. chervil
1	med. head cauliflower, in flowerettes
1	10 oz. pkg. frozen green beans, thawed out
1	10 oz. pkg. frozen green peas, thawed out
1-2	tsp. salt
	Parsley

In a deep, heavy skillet or pot, brown the chops in their own fat, making sure they're well done on both sides, prodding them with a fork in the beginning to prevent them from sticking. When brown, add the potatoes and carrots, together with spices, herbs, salt and pepper; tuck the bouillon cube in and pour vermouth and water over all. Bring to a slow boil, reduce heat, and simmer, covered, for 40 minutes. Add the beans, peas and cauliflower, check for salt, and simmer covered for another 20 minutes.

Sprinkle parsley on top and serve with rolls and a chilled bottle of white wine.

PARTY CHOPS
(4 Servings)

2	tbs. butter or margarine
4	leeks, in 1″ pieces
6	lean pork chops
12	fresh mushrooms, washed and quartered
3	med.-large tomatoes, in wedges
1	tsp. salt
½	tsp. black pepper
½	tsp. sweet basil
¼	tsp. fenugreek or curry powder
½	tsp. thyme
¼	tsp. marjoram
½	cup light cream
¼	cup dry sherry
6	slices of bacon cut in half crosswise
	Parmesan cheese

In an ovenproof dish, brown the chops well on both sides in their own fat, prodding them a little to prevent sticking. Remove chops from pot, melt butter and sauté the leeks, for about 5 minutes. Place the chops on top, distribute the mushrooms over them, tuck the tomato wedges in and sprinkle all with salt, pepper and herbs before pouring cream and sherry over all. Cover and bake in a 350° oven for 45 minutes.

Remove cover, arrange bacon slices on top and sprinkle generously with Parmesan cheese. Return to oven, uncovered, and continue baking for another 15 minutes.

Serve with crusty bread, a crisp green salad and a dry red wine.

In fixing rice, I usually follow the Greek method of simmering it for 30 minutes, stirring once. In the follow-

ing recipe, you can bake the rice for 1 hour without
having to check it. If it should stick a tiny bit—which it
never has for me—just quote from Cervantes' *Don Qui-
xote:* "They had best not stir the rice, though it sticks to
the pot . . ." and the outcome is justified.

NOTES

RICEY PORK CHOPS
(6 Servings)

6	**rib pork chops**
1	**cup diced celery**
1	**med. onion, chopped**
1	**can tomato soup**
1	**cup water**
1	**tsp. salt**
1	**tsp. oregano**
½	**tsp. crumbled bay leaves**
1	**tsp. dry mustard**
1	**1 lb. can okra**
1	**1 lb. can red kidney beans**
1	**12 oz. can whole kernel corn**
¾	**cup ripe olives, sliced**
1	**cup raw rice**

In a large pot or kettle, brown the pork chops well on both sides in their own fat, moving them around a little at first to prevent from sticking. Set aside; add the onion and celery to the pork drippings and sauté for about 5 minutes. Stir in the tomato soup, water, salt and herbs; heat to boiling and add the undrained canned vegetables together with the sliced olives and rice. Mix everything very well, place the chops on top, cover and bake in a 350° oven for 1 hour.

Serve with Ry-Krisp, a green salad and a glass of beer.

This is truly a full meal and needs to be followed by nothing but a good strong cup of coffee, but do make sure it's strong so that nobody will have to quote that famous line from *Punch:* "Look here—Steward—if this is coffee, I want tea; but if this is tea, then I wish for coffee."

WINTER PORK CHOPS
(4 Servings)

6	lean pork chops
2	tbs. butter or margarine
4	med. potatoes, pared and quartered
1	cup water
2	6 oz. cans tomato paste
1	cup half and half
1	tsp. salt
¼	tsp. black pepper
1	tsp. dill
1	10 oz. pkg. frozen peas

Melt the butter in a deep skillet and brown the chops well on both sides. Remove chops from skillet; add and brown the quartered potatoes stirring all the time. Add the chops, tomato sauce, salt, pepper and dill and pour water over all, giving it a good stir. Bring to a boil, reduce heat and simmer, covered, for 45 minutes. Add the frozen peas and cream and continue simmering for another 15 minutes. If you feel the mixture is too juicy, leave the cover off during this last stage.

Serve with dinner rolls and a green salad.

This last pork recipe draws on the Hungarian kitchen for its inspiration. It's the kind of dish that takes the edge off a raw, chilly winter evening.

PORK AND KRAUT A LA BUDAPEST
(4-6 Servings)

2	large onions, sliced
2	tbs. butter or margarine
2	lbs. pork, in 1″ cubes
1	tsp. salt
3	tsp. paprika
1	tsp. caraway seed
1	large can light beer
2	1 lb. cans sauerkraut, drained
1	cup commercial sour cream

In your Dutch oven, melt the butter and slowly sauté the onion until translucent, about 5 minutes. Add the pork, sprinkle with salt, and let the browning of the meat progress slowly, stirring constantly. Sprinkle the mixture with paprika and caraway seed. Add half the beer; cover, and simmer for 45 minutes, stirring occasionally and adding the remaining beer as needed. Stir in the drained sauerkraut and simmer for another 15 minutes or until the kraut is well heated. Then add the sour cream, letting that just heat up a little before you serve with slices of seeded rye bread, unsalted butter and cold, cold beer.

VEAL

Did you know that Shakespeare's father was a butcher and that as a teen-ager William plied the family trade?

According to inquisitive, contemporary neighbors, it is reported that to this task as well he brought his flair for the dramatic. When young William killed a calf, he would do it in high style, making a speech.

Knowing the effort that went into presenting the customers with their preferred cuts might have led Shakespeare years later to write in *King Lear:* "A knave, a rascal, an eater of broken meats."

If you have limited your veal cooking repertoire to an occasional weiner schnitzel or breaded cutlet, try at least a few of the following recipes. You may be surprised to discover the fun and flavorful things other nationalities have thought up in serving that delicate meat.

CHINESE VEAL
(4 Servings)

1	lb. veal, in strips
1	heart of celery, in ½" pieces
4-6	scallions, 1" pieces
2	tbs. butter or margarine
½	tsp. salt *or to taste*
¼	tsp. black pepper
¼	tsp. ground ginger
1	can chicken broth
¼	cup soy sauce
½	cup raw rice
8	mushrooms, cleaned, sliced
1	cup peas
½	cup sliced almonds

In the melted butter sauté the veal strips, celery and scallion pieces for about 5-10 minutes, stirring occasionally. Sprinkle the mixture with salt, pepper and ginger; pour the chicken broth and soy sauce over, bring to a boil; add the rice, reduce heat, cover and let simmer for 15 minutes. Stir in mushrooms and peas, check whether it's gingery enough for you, re-cover and continue simmering for another 15 minutes.

Sprinkle the almonds on top, and serve with cucumber slices prevalent in your green salad.

FRENCH GREEN PEPPER VEAL DISH
(4-6 Servings)

1½	lbs. lean veal, cubed
½	lb. lean pork, cubed
3	tbs. butter or margarine
2	large onions, chopped
4	green peppers, in ¼″ strips
4	tomatoes, sliced
2	tbs. minced parsley
1	tsp. fennel seed, crushed
½	tsp. sweet basil
1	clove garlic, crushed
1-2	tsp. salt
¼	tsp. white pepper
1	cup commercial sour cream

In a deep baking dish or casserole, heat the butter and quickly brown the cubed meat well on all sides over high heat turning it constantly. Reduce heat and add the chopped onions, pushing the meat aside while you sauté the onions until translucent, about 5 minutes. Remove the pot from the heat; mix the meats and onions, stir in the pepper strips, arrange the tomato slices on top, sprinkle with salt, pepper, garlic and herbs, cover tightly and bake in a 350° oven for about 1 hour. Take the dish from the oven, spread the sour cream on top and place it under the boiler, uncovered, for 2-3 minutes.

Serve with breadsticks and a chilled vin rosé, followed by a piece of your favorite cheese cake.

This next dish is truly different in texture and flavor, but deserves a try in spite of its unorthodox ingredients.

HAITIAN STYLE VEAL
(4-6 Servings)

3	lbs. veal, cubed
1	tsp. salt
½	tsp. black pepper
4	tbs. butter or margarine
3	large tomatoes, in wedges
2	med. onions, chopped
1	tsp. allspice
½	tsp. ginger
¼	tsp. coriander
¾	cup water
¼	cup dry white wine
2	small cans cashew nuts

Sprinkle the cubed veal with salt and pepper, heat the butter in the pot and brown veal well on all sides. Add the tomatoes and onions, sautéing them for about 5 minutes. Sprinkle spices over all, stir in nuts, and pour in wine and water. Bring to a boil, reduce heat and let simmer for 1 hour, checking for moisture now and then.

Serve with a tart, crisp green salad and crusty French bread.

If you think it sounds or reads a little outlandish, just remember Aristotle's words: "Change in all things is sweet" . . . and I am referring to the Greek philosopher, not the shipping magnate.

Like most children I went through a period where I'd heap more food on my plate than I could eat, obviously taking my cue from Dixon Merritt's limerick:

> *A wonderful bird is the pelican,*
> *His bill will hold more than his belican.*
> *He can take in his beak*
> *Food enough for a week,*
> *But I'm damned if I see how the helican.*

I never discovered the pelican's secret, a fact I bitterly grieved, especially if we were having Veal Birds for dinner —my childhood favorite.

The following recipe takes a little time to prepare, but every minute is worth it.

HOLLAND STYLE VEAL BIRDS
(4-6 Servings)

½	lb. lean ground beef
1	egg, beaten
1	tsp. salt
½	tsp. dried dill weed
½	tsp. pepper
6	gherkins, diced
2-3	hard-boiled eggs, sliced
2	lbs. thin veal scallops
4	tbs. butter or margarine
3	med. onions, sliced
4	med. potatoes, pared and quartered
3	large carrots, in chunks
1	tsp. salt
1	can consomme or beef broth
½	cup dry white wine

Mix together the ground beef, beaten egg, 1 tsp. salt, pepper, dill and diced gherkins. Divide this mixture evenly among the veal scallops, placing a slice of hard-boiled egg in the center of the meat mixture before you roll up your "birds." Secure the "birds" with either string or toothpicks, and put aside while you prepare the vegetables.

In a pot melt the butter, sauté onions until translucent, about 5 minutes; push the onions aside and brown the "birds" evenly on all sides. You might have to do this in two steps. Place the browned "birds" on the onions, tuck the pieces of potato and carrot in among the meat, sprinkle with rest of salt, and pour consomme and wine over it all. Bring to a boil, reduce heat and let simmer for 30-40 minutes under cover.

Serve with dinner rolls, a bib-lettuce and cherry-tomato salad and chilled white wine, and you have a delightful meal, delicate in flavor and texture.

This next recipe is one you can fix rather quickly. The friend who gave it to me added garlic, which I omit . . . but that you'll have to decide for yourself.

NOTES

ITALIAN VEAL CHOPS
(3-4 Servings)

1½	lbs. veal chops
2	tbs. butter
4	tbs. olive oil
1	celery heart, sliced
2	carrots, chopped
¼	tsp. crushed rosemary
1	med. onion, chopped
1	tsp. parsley chopped
¾	cup dry sherry
2	med. tomatoes, in wedges
1	tsp. salt
½	tsp. pepper
	Canned shoestring potatoes

After you've prepared the vegetables, using only the inner part of the heart of celery, melt the butter in a deep skillet, heat with olive oil and brown the chops well on both sides. Add the chopped vegetables, salt, pepper, parsley and rosemary. Stir, cover and simmer for about 10 minutes. Then stir in the sherry and continue simmering under cover for 20 minutes, giving the dish an occasional stir.

Serve with canned shoestring potatoes you've heated in a low, low oven or garlic bread if that's your preference. A chilled vin rosé with this is not bad either.

In 1750, Lord Chesterfield wrote in a letter: "Paris is the place in the world where, if you please, you may best unite the *utile* and the *dulce*." Interpreting *utile* as necessary and *dulce* as pleasant, one can say that his combination has been carried over into Parisian cooking. In this next recipe, everyday ingredients are turned into a feast.

PARISIAN VEAL STEW
(4-6 Servings)

2	tbs. flour
½	tsp. poultry seasoning
3	lbs. boneless veal, cubed
4	tbs. butter or margarine
½	tsp. crumbled bay leaves
⅛	tsp. ground cloves
¼	tsp. allspice
12	small white onions, peeled
4	med. carrots, in chunks
1	10 oz. pkg. frozen peas
1	can chicken broth
½	cup heavy cream
2	egg yolks
2	tbs. lemon juice

Mix the flour and poultry seasoning in a paper bag, and dust the cubed veal in this before browning it well on all sides in hot butter. Reduce heat and add the whole white onions, sautéing them for about 5 minutes. Sprinkle the herbs and spices, with salt to taste, over the mixture; pour chicken broth over all, cover and simmer for 1 hour. Now add the carrots and peas and continue simmering for another 30 minutes.

Combine the cream with the beaten egg yolks and lemon juice, mix in a little of the liquid from the pot and add this to the pot. Heat to just below boiling point, being very careful the egg doesn't curdle.

Serve with marinated tomato slices—try and substitute brandy for vinegar some time—hard crust rolls and a chilled vin rosé.

Oh, one more thing. Try and have the right number of

people for dinner when you serve this. Because of the egg, it doesn't reheat very well—if at all.

This next dish is bound to please whatever youngsters you may have in your family or among your friends. You don't have to master the art of twirling spaghetti around your fork—only to see it fall off halfway to your mouth —and you don't have to worry about reheating this sturdy dish.

NOTES

VEAL RISOTTO
(4-6 Servings)

2	lbs. boneless veal, 1″ cubes
¼	lb. Italian sausage
1	large onion, thinly sliced
2	tbs. olive oil
4	tbs. butter or margarine
1	1 lb. can tomatoes
2½	cups chicken broth
1	cup raw rice
1-2	tsp. salt
½	tsp. pepper
½	tsp. sweet basil
¼	tsp. oregano
2	tbs. parsley flakes
¼	cup grated Romano cheese
	Romano or Parmesan cheese

In a large pot, heat the butter and olive oil and brown the cubed veal well on all sides. Remove from pan temporarily, reduce heat and add the thinly sliced onion together with the diced sausage. Let the onion and sausage cook for about 5 minutes, stirring to prevent sticking. Return the browned veal to the pot, pour in tomatoes and chicken broth, sprinkle with salt, pepper and herbs, bring to a boil and stir in rice. Cover and simmer for 15 minutes. Give the mixture another good stir, re-cover, and continue simmering for 15 minutes.

Just before you serve, stir in the grated Romano cheese and have more of that or of Parmesan on hand for those who might want to sprinkle it on top of their individual helping.

Serve with a crisp, green salad and garlic bread, and you have done your share to overcome the generation gap.

We all know from the TV commercials that some men, in judging women, start with the hair and presumably work their way down, while others start with the legs and, at least visually, never get any further.

But did you also know that there are men who go practically out of their minds if you mention quadruped legs, such as shanks? If the man in your life belongs in this category, try the following recipe, and Ambrose Bierce's tart statement that: "Woman would be more charming if one could fall into her arms without falling into her hands . . ." will be completely obliterated from his mind.

VEAL SHANKS ITALIENNE
(4-6 Servings)

8	2″ pieces veal shank, about 4 lbs.
4	tbs. flour
1-2	tsp. salt
½	tsp. pepper
4	tbs. olive oil
1	onion, chopped
1	clove garlic, minced
1	tsp. oregano
½	tsp. rosemary
2	tbs. tomato paste
1	tbs. lemon juice
1	can chicken broth
½	cup dry white wine
4	carrots, pared, in chunks
6	small white onions, peeled
2	celery stalks, 1″ pieces
4	med. potatoes, pared and quartered
1	tbs. parsley

Mix flour, salt and pepper and coat the pieces of meat in this. In a large pot or kettle, heat the oil and brown the shanks well on all sides. Remove shanks temporarily, add the chopped onion and garlic to the pot and sauté for about 5 minutes or until onion is translucent. Place the shanks back in the pot, sprinkle with oregano and rosemary; spoon the tomato paste over and pour lemon juice, broth and wine over all. Give it a light stir; bring to a boil, reduce heat and let simmer, covered, for 1 hour while you prepare the vegetables.

When the hour is up add the vegetables and the parsley, stir well; cover and simmer for another 30 minutes until vegetables are done and the meat is tender but still hanging onto the bones.

Have a tart green salad ready as well as sourdough bread and a bottle of chilled white wine, and everything will be perfect for your guy.

This last veal dish is a more festive variation of the standard meatballs and can easily be made out of staples you most likely have on hand. It definitely calls for a salad in my opinion, but then I'm the type who could eat wilted salad for breakfast, totally ignoring Cervantes' statement: "Not with whom thou art bred, but with whom thou art fed . . ." as a key to my character.

SWEDISH VEAL BALLS WITH POPPY TOP
(6 Servings)

1½	lbs. ground veal
¾	cup bread crumbs
1	egg, beaten
2	tbs. parsley flakes
1	tsp. salt
¼	tsp. white pepper
¼	tsp. paprika
¼	tsp. mace
1	16 oz. can white onions
1	7 oz. can mushrooms
1	can chicken broth
1	cup dairy sour cream

POPPY TOP

2	cups Bisquick
1½	tsp. poppy seeds
½	tsp. celery salt
¾	cup milk

Mix veal, bread crumbs, egg, parsley and spices in a medium-size bowl, blending everything well, and shape into approximately 18 balls. Place the balls in a generously buttered large baking dish and arrange the onions and mushrooms around them. Combine, in the bowl you used for fixing the meatballs, the sour cream with the chicken broth and liquid from mushrooms, and pour into baking dish. Bake in a 375° oven for 40 minutes.

When the time is almost up, mix all ingredients for the topping; roll out on a floured surface, place over baking dish, cut a few slits for steam to escape and return to oven for another 10-15 minutes, this time at 475°. The dish will be ready when the top is nice and golden.

VARIETY MEATS

There's an old Latin proverb that says: "No pleasure endures unseasoned by variety . . ." so before closing, let me give you a couple of recipes, favorites of mine and not usually found on anybody's menu.

Contrary to most people's thinking, chicken livers can be served in more ways than chopped, a theory I hope you will adopt after trying the next two recipes.

CHINESE CHICKEN LIVERS
(3-4 Servings)

2-3	tbs. butter or margarine
3	large green onions, ½″ pieces
1	1″ piece ginger root, peeled and minced
1	green pepper, seeded and chopped
1	carrot, pared and chopped
1	small head cauliflower, broken into flowerettes
6	Chinese mushrooms, soaked in water
1	lb. chicken livers, cut into thin slices
1	tbs. soy sauce
1	tbs. dry red wine
	Salt *to taste*
	Chinese noodles

Heat 1 tbs. of the butter in a deep skillet; add the onions and ginger and sauté until onions are tender and translucent, being careful not to brown them. Set aside on a plate and start adding the other vegetables . . . one at a time . . . sautéing them individually in butter until about half done and setting them aside, winding up with the soaked mushrooms, snipped into little pieces. Remove those from skillet as well, turn up the heat and quickly sauté the sliced chicken livers in whatever butter you have left. Now add all the precooked vegetables to the skillet, give it a slight stir, season with soy sauce, red wine and salt, heat through, and serve. Chinese noodles go along with this nicely.

Even youngsters who might have an inclination against livers will like them in this Italian-inspired dish.

CHICKEN LIVER RISOTTO
(3-4 Servings)

12	mushrooms, washed and quartered
1	lb. chicken livers
4	tbs. butter or margarine
1	small onion, chopped
1	tsp. salt
¼	tsp. pepper
½	tsp. thyme
½	tsp. sweet basil
¼	tsp. marjoram
1	tbs. parsley flakes
1½	cups tomato juice
2	med. tomatoes, chopped
1	cup water
1	beef bouillon cube
¼	cup dry sherry
1	cup raw rice

Melt the butter or margarine and sauté the mushrooms for about 5 minutes. Put aside and quickly, lightly brown the chicken livers. Put aside with the mushrooms.

Add to the pot the chopped onion and sauté until translucent, then stir in herbs, salt, pepper and tomato pieces, letting it simmer for 2-3 minutes. Pour in the tomato juice, water, sherry, add the bouillon cube, stir and bring to a boil before you stir in the rice. Reduce heat, cover and simmer for 15 minutes, then add the sautéed mushrooms and chicken livers. Give it all a good stir, cover and let simmer for another 15 minutes.

Serve with a crisp green salad, garlic bread and a dry red wine, and you won't hear any complaints from anybody.

If you thought sweetbreads were for ladies' luncheons only, let me prove you wrong. They make for a very tasty dinner dish that'll do any man proud. The actual cooking doesn't take long, but you should allow time for soaking and cleaning the sweetbreads in advance.

NOTES

SWEETBREADS CHAUSSEUR
(2-3 Servings)

2	pairs sweetbreads, cleaned and cut in bite-size pieces
1	tbs. lemon juice
½	cup olive oil
½	tsp. salt *or to taste*
¼	tsp. pepper
2	large tomatoes, in wedges
1	small onion, chopped
1	green pepper, seeded and chopped
1	red pepper, seeded and chopped
½	lb. mushrooms, washed and sliced
½	tsp. sweet basil
¼	tsp. rosemary, crushed
¼	cup dry sherry
	Flour

Soak the sweetbreads in cold water for 2 hours. Drain and pour boiling water over them, adding the lemon juice to this. Let stand for 10 minutes, then drain, peel and remove all membranes. Cut into large bite-size pieces.

When you're ready to cook, roll the sweetbreads in flour while you heat the oil in the pot. Add the sweetbreads and cook until they have a nice brown crust. Remove from pot, add all the vegetables; sprinkle with salt, pepper and herbs and sauté for about 5-10 minutes, making sure the vegetables don't get too well done. Put the sweetbreads back in the pot, give all a good stir, pour the sherry over and let simmer without cover over low flame until everything is heated through and most of the liquid has evaporated, about 10 minutes.

Serve with cucumber salad, dinner rolls and a chilled bottle of vin rosé.

Milton Berle is quoted as saying: "A committee is a group that keeps minutes and loses hours . . ." so if you decide to serve the next recipe, don't ask your family or friends if they'd like it or would care to try it; simply serve this much-maligned piece of meat and marvel at the reaction you will get.

I should warn you, though, removing the skin from the tongue is not the easiest job in the world and does require a little time and work. Also plan on pre-preparation time.

NOTES

POTTED TONGUE
(4 Servings)

1	smoked beef tongue, about 4 lbs.
4	tbs. butter or margarine
3	onions, sliced
3	large carrots, scraped and sliced
1	celery heart, inner part only, ½" pieces
4	large tomatoes, in wedges
½	tsp. salt
¼	tsp. black pepper
½	tsp. thyme
½	tsp. sweet basil
¼	tsp. marjoram
½	cup dry white wine
1	cup water
1	beef bouillon cube
2	10 oz. pkg. frozen lima beans, thawed out
1	2 oz. can sliced, ripe olives

The day before or early in the morning, put the tongue in the pot and cover with water; bring to a quick boil, reduce heat and let boil for 2 hours. When the meat is cool enough to handle, trim off all roots and tubes with a sharp knife and make an indentation with the point of the knife under the tongue, cutting through the thick skin. Carefully peel off all skin; if necessary chip away with the knife to remove it all. When that's done, you're ready to start cooking.

In a large pot or Dutch oven, melt the butter and brown the tongue on all sides. Remove temporarily from pot while you sauté the sliced onion and carrots in the butter, reducing the heat for this. When done, in about 5-10 minutes, put the tongue back on this bed of vegetables, tuck the tomato wedges in around and on top of the tongue, sprinkle with salt, pepper and herbs, cut the bouillon cube into quarters and place among the tomatoes before pouring the wine and water over all. Cover and simmer for 1 hour, then add mushrooms, lima beans and olives, stirring them in lightly. Cover and continue simmering for another 20 minutes.

Lift the tongue out on a platter, carve into thin slices and serve with the vegetables right from the pot. Serve with crescent-type dinner rolls and a chilled vin rosé, and you have a truly delectable meal that'll make a convert out of anybody.

NOTES

EPILOGUE

Jean Cocteau once said: "Mirrors should reflect a little before throwing back images."

This is a gentle, beautiful thought I kept in mind while compiling this book, because as in a mirror, some of the self is reflected in the cooking.

In the final analysis, the preparation of food lives up to Thomas Edison's statement: "Genius is one per cent inspiration and ninety-nine per cent perspiration."

Maybe my attitude is best summed up in the words of Logan Pearsall Smith: "There are two things to aim at in life: first, to get what you want; and, after that, to enjoy it. Only the wisest of mankind achieve the second."